Serving the Academic, Social, and Emotional Needs of Multicultural Newcomers

Serving the Academic, Social, and Emotional Needs of Multicultural Newcomers

Brenda Custodio and Judith B. O'Loughlin

University of Michigan Press
Ann Arbor

Copyright © 2025 by the University of Michigan
All rights reserved
Published in the United States of America by the
University of Michigan Press
Manufactured in the United States of America

Printed on acid-free paper

ISBN 978-0-472-03988-3 (print)
ISBN 978-0-472-22217-9 (e-book)

First published January 2025

No part of this publication may be reproduced, stored in a retrieval system, or transmitted in any form or by any means, electronic, mechanical, or otherwise, without the written permission of the publisher.

Contents

List of Figures	viii
List of Tables	ix
List of Acronyms	x
Foreword	xii
Roger C. Rosenthal, Executive Director, Migrant Legal Action Program, Washington, DC.	
Introduction	1
Why Do We Need a Book about Newcomers?	1
Who Are Our Newcomers?	2
Where Are Our Newcomers Coming From?	4
What Needs Do Newcomers Bring to Our Classrooms?	7
Self-Study or Group Study Activities	8
Five Best Practices	9
1: Newcomer Program Designs and Variations	11
Best Practice Number One: Collaborate with school/district professionals to create a program specifically to meet the unique needs of your new arrivals.	11
History of Newcomer Programs	12
Program Design Considerations	13
Critical Components of a Newcomer Program	17
Low Incidence Programs	19
Elementary Programs	21
Secondary Programs	22
Programming for Older Teens	25
Programs for Students with Limited or Interrupted Formal Education (SLIFE or SIFE)	25
Newcomers with Disabilities	27
Newcomers Who Are Gifted and/or Talented	28

Newcomer Programs for Adults ... 29
The US Department of Education Newcomer Toolkit ... 31
Self-Study or Group Study Activities ... 32

2: Academic Supports for Newcomers ... 35

Best Practice Number Two: Provide intensive literacy, numeracy, and content area support, especially for students with interrupted schooling. ... 35

Literacy Development for Newcomers ... 35
Critical Components of a Literacy Program for Newcomers ... 36
    Phonemic Awareness ... 36
    Letter Knowledge/ Alphabetics ... 37
    Phonics, Decoding, Word Work ... 38
    Concepts of Print ... 39
    Knowledge of Text Structure ... 39
    Fluency ... 41
    Oral language ... 41
    Language Structures and Conventions ... 42
    Vocabulary and Background Knowledge ... 42
    Comprehension ... 43
    Cross-Language Connections ... 44
    Writing ... 44
    The Reading Rope ... 44
Literacy Instruction ... 46
Numeracy Development for Newcomers ... 46
    The Myth of "Math Is Universal" ... 47
    Word Problems ... 48
    Tips for Solving Word Problems ... 48
Teaching Numeracy to Newcomers ... 49
Teaching Content to Newcomers ... 50
    Think-Pair-Share-Square Example ... 50
Self-Study or Group Study Activities ... 51

3: Instructional Strategies and Classroom Activities for Newcomers ... 53

Best Practice Number Three: Develop the classroom supports necessary for students to achieve academic success. ... 53

Welcoming New Students ... 53
    Where to Begin Instruction ... 53
    Checklist for Welcoming Students ... 54
    The Hidden Curriculum ... 55

Supporting Students' Cultures: How to Be a Culturally Proficient
   Teacher of Newcomers 58
Progression of Instruction Based on Language Proficiency 59
Instructional Strategies and Supports for New Arrivals 60
   Build upon Prior Knowledge 60
   Teach Language and Content Simultaneously 61
   Employ Graphic Organizers 62
   Utilize Peer Assistance and Group Work 62
   Focus on Vocabulary 63
   Use Accommodations and Modifications 66
   Apply the Gradual Release of Responsibility Model 67
   Promote Translanguaging 67
   Teach to Standards 68
Co-Teaching for Newcomers 69
   English Learner Co-Teaching Configurations 70
Assessment: Showcasing Student Growth through
   Multiple Measures of Data 72
Self-Study or Group Study Activities 73

4: Physical, Social, Emotional, and Educational Supports for Newcomers 75
   Best Practice Number Four: Provide supports that address the physical,
      social, emotional, and educational challenges of newcomers. 75
   Newcomers Who Are Dually Identified 77
   Utilizing Multi-Tiered Systems of Support (MTSS) for Newcomers 77
      Components of MTSS 80
   Addressing Student Physical, Social, and Emotional Needs 82
   Staffing a Newcomer Program 83
      The Importance of a Trained Staff 83
   Self-Study or Group Study Activities 90

5: Family and Community Supports 93
   Best Practice Number Five: Work with families and communities
      to support students outside of the school environment. 93
   Developing and Sustaining Family Partnerships 94
   Collaborating with Community Organizations 97
   How Community Organizations Can Support Newcomers 97
   How to Get Connected to Community Organizations 99
   Self-Study or Group Study Activities 99

References and Resources 101
Index 107

List of Figures

Figure 1	Academic and Social-Emotional Issues for Newcomers	8
Figure 2	Critical Components of a Newcomer Program	17
Figure 3	Plot Line	40
Figure 4	The Reading Rope	45
Figure 5	Progression of Instruction Based on Language Proficiency	59
Figure 6	Gradual Release of Responsibility Model	67
Figure 7	Response to Intervention (RTI) Model	79

List of Tables

Table 1	Components of an Orientation Program	32
Table 2	Soft Skills for Adult Newcomers	33
Table 3	A-Z Vocabulary List	38
Table 4	Plot Chart	40
Table 5	Non-Fiction Text Information	41
Table 6	Components of a Literacy Program	51
Table 7	Checklist for Welcoming Newcomers	54
Table 8	KWL Chart	61
Table 9	Multiple-Meaning or Polysemous Words Chart	63
Table 10	Common Spanish Cognates Chart	65
Table 11	Typical Accommodations and Modifications	66
Table 12	Language Difference or Language Disorder	78
Table 13	Accommodations and Modifications for English Learners with Special Needs	81
Table 14	Administrator Classroom Observation Checklist	85

List of Acronyms

CUNY	City College of New York
CVC words	Consonant-vowel-consonant words (e.g., "bat," "dog," "hot")
EAL	English as an additional language
EFL	English as a foreign language
EL	English learner
ELD	English language development
ELO	Expanded learning opportunity
ELPA21	English Language Proficiency Assessment for the 21st Century
ESL	English as a second language
ESOL	English for speakers of other languages
ESSA	Every Student Succeeds Act
FAFSA	Free Application for Federal Student Aid
GED	General education diploma
GO	Graphic organizer
GPA	Grade point average
GT	Gifted and talented
IDEA	Individuals with Disabilities Education Act
IELCE	Integrated English Literacy and Civics Education program
K-12	Students in grades kindergarten through twelfth grade span
KWL chart	A chart to describe what the learner knows, wants to know, and has learned
L1	First or home language
LEA	Local education agency or school district
ML	Multilingual learner
NES	Native English speaker
OCR	Office of Civil Rights
PreK-12	Students in a pre-kindergarten class through to twelfth grade span
MPI	Migrant Policy Institute
MTSS	Multi-tiered systems of support
NAGC	National Association for Gifted Children

PD	Professional development
RTI	Response to intervention
SDAIE	Specially designed academic instruction in English
SEA	State Education Agency
SEL	Social-emotional learning
SIFE	Students with interrupted formal education
SIOP	Sheltered Instruction Observation Protocol
SLIFE	Students with limited and/or interrupted formal education
TESOL	Teachers of English to Speakers of Other Languages
Tiers 1, 2, 3	Levels of instructional intervention
TPR	Total physical response
TPS	Temporary protected status
UNHCR	United Nations High Commissioner for Refugees
USDE	United States Department of Education
WIOA	Workforce Innovation and Opportunity Act of 2014

Foreword

Much of my life's work as an attorney and an advocate has focused on the rights of immigrant children and English learners in the public schools. I have worked on a myriad of issues regarding enrollment in school and access to school activities. I have also worked on the individual rights of students not proficient in English and their parents.

In my work over the years, I have seen substantial growth in the diversity in public schools. If a retired teacher or administrator would return to their school after a 25-year absence, they would be very surprised to see the changing demographics in their school and school district. This growth has occurred in many places. Certain regions and states have seen a dramatic growth in students who were born in other countries and students who are not proficient in English. Rural areas have also seen very dramatic change, but so have many cities whose diversity has increased, as well as states where there was already a diverse population. Some school districts have as many as 100 or more languages identified through their home language surveys as the first language of their students. Further, with the growth in the diversity of the school population, there are still some schools with a low incidence of English learners or a low incidence of students whose first language is different from other English learners.

Schools have also seen, many for the first time, students with interrupted educations, some for short, interrupted periods and some for lengthy times. As one who has worked for many years with the mobile migratory farmworker student community, I have seen the enormous impact that such interruptions and disruptions (notably two different concepts) have had on students' academic performance as well as on their self-esteem and mental health. Students might think of themselves as not capable of achieving good grades in school because they struggle to overcome their interrupted and disrupted schooling or have difficulty learning English. They consequently might be dealing with a low self-image. "Am I really never going to get good grades? Maybe I should just drop out and work to support my family."

There are many challenges these days in the field of education. But there are also many opportunities for fulfilling work that makes an enormous difference to a student.

In my work as an advocate, I am constantly amazed at the generosity that many teachers show toward their students, as well as the creativity of many administrators. But, sadly, I also find situations where differences among students (differences that are not the choice of a student) are not appreciated or respected. In some situations, either through neglect or intentions, some students are not treated fairly or equally.

Some of those immutable characteristics that students bring with them include race, national origin, gender, English language proficiency, disability, citizenship, nationality, income, age, mobility, living environments, the status of being housed or not, and immigration status. These are all characteristics that need to be anticipated and planned for by schools in order to ensure students are afforded an equal opportunity to learn. In order to properly accommodate the diversity of characteristics that students present, there needs to be a full understanding of these characteristics and how educational institutions need to respond to them. This all can be a tall order.

This valuable book focuses on those recently arrived in the United States. These students will vary enormously in their educational status and preparation, including students with interrupted formal education (SIFE). Many SIFE present a good number of the characteristics that are listed above. On top of those characteristics, they have missed a continuous exposure to formal education. Often that interrupted education is the result of traumatic events in their lives or that occurred in their family.

The book treats many issues that are important for educators to consider when working with the new demographically diverse student population. There is much of value here that transcends working with just the newcomers in a school district. The book presents a wide variety of situations that apply to newcomers, but many of these situations also occur among non-newcomer English learners, and even in the general student population. The book also provides valuable and thoughtful exercises to assist in the planning and execution of education for the newcomer population.

Ensuring that all students have access to quality education strengthens our communities and our country. A solid education for students of all backgrounds and experiences provides both economic and social benefits to our society.

I strongly recommend that educators consider the issues raised in this valuable book.

Roger C. Rosenthal
Executive Director
Migrant Legal Action Program
Washington, DC

Introduction

Why Do We Need a Book about Newcomers?

The term "newcomers" in the second language field refers to recent immigrants, most of whom qualify to receive English language services. This term describes students based solely on their length of time in the country, but their educational and personal needs are as varied as their backgrounds. It is these needs that shall be the focus of this book.

We are defining newcomers as students who have attended US schools less than two years, with a focus on those students who began attending at grades 3 and above. We understand that students who arrive during the primary grades of K-2 may also need assistance, especially with oral English, beginning reading and writing, mathematics, and school routines, but the larger academic gaps begin to appear in the intermediate grades, and the gaps become chasms at the middle and high school level. Newcomers often require academic, social, and/or emotional supports that may not be available in a typical English as a second language (ESL) or bilingual program. This book will look at who these students are, describe the types of programming and services that may best serve their needs, and consider how schools can work together with community organizations to provide a comprehensive network of support.

It is our desire that by the end of this book the reader will have gained an overview of the diverse linguistic and academic backgrounds of newcomer students, obtained additional strategies and resources for supporting these students in both language and content classes, and discovered new pathways to more effectively collaborate with the families and the broader community in which they live.

The Migration Policy Institute (MPI) has indicated that "the increase in the number of immigrant-background children in US schools over the last decade has challenged K-12 educators to expand their capacity to serve students who may have unique characteristics and particular needs" (Sugarman, October 2023). Their fall 2023 fact sheet, *Recent Immigrant Children: A Profile of New Arrivals to U.S. Schools,* indicates that:

- Half of the immigrant children who arrived in 2021 were Latino, with the second largest group being Asian American and Pacific Islanders
- Among the recently arrived 14–17-year-old youths, nine percent were not enrolled in school and had not completed high school.

As MPI notes, English learners, but more specifically newcomers, are a growing population of English learners in the United States. The percentage of recent arrivals rose from 15% to 20% of the total English learner (EL) population in the last decade, with the majority continuing to settle in the traditional border areas and cities, but increasing numbers are also moving into the suburbs, rural areas, and other non-traditional locales. Many school districts are searching for practices and programs to support these students and their families, to promote their academic success, and to keep them in school until high school graduation. It is our desire that educators find suggestions and solutions in this book to help create classrooms that are welcoming and supportive to the students' personal needs while also being strategic in meeting their academic needs.

Who Are Our Newcomers?

In a study on newcomers conducted by Deborah Short and Beverly Boyson for the Center for Applied Linguistics entitled *Helping Newcomer Students Succeed in Secondary Schools and Beyond* (2012), the authors found that newcomers fell into three main categories: students with strong educational backgrounds before arriving in the United States, students with some educational disruption, and students who have little or no prior education. The number and type of students present in your school/district will affect the type of programming and services these students will need.

Students who were attending school on a regular basis before moving to the United States usually will need the least amount of specialized programming. Some of these students will have studied English before arrival and may have attended a school in which the curriculum was like that found in the United States. For these students, a short orientation to their new school may be sufficient, but life in a new country will still provide some culture shock for both the students and their family. For these students, in addition to specialized English language instruction, a "buddy" may help the new student through the initial transition.

For students with some educational background, trying to catch up to their peers who are ahead of them academically can lead to frustration. With support, including sheltered and/or bilingual courses, these students should be able to close the academic gap in two or three years. For many of these students, one of the biggest barriers they face may be hearing and using English for hours at a time. Even for those students who arrive with some English skills, the process of mentally translating from their native language (we use "native," "home," and "first language" interchangeably in our writing) to English for extended time periods can lead to daily headaches. They may reach their limit before the final bell rings and simply tune out some of the class or even some of the day. When bilingual programming is not available, it may be months before students are really understanding most of what is happening in the classes. Sometimes, just giving them a chance for some quiet time during the day will help during this adjustment period.

The final category, students with intermittent or severely interrupted educational backgrounds, known as students with interrupted formal education (SIFE) or students with limited or interrupted formal education (SLIFE), will require the most intensive special services. Most of these students come from political and/or economic situations that prevented them from attending school on a regular basis. These disruptions were often accompanied by traumatic experiences that continue to impact a student's ability to focus and perform academic tasks. Programming to address social and emotional issues as well as help with closing the academic gaps will be necessary for academic progress. We will focus on supports for this group of learners in Chapter Two.

Regardless of previous educational level, most newcomers, even those students with an uninterrupted education, do not arrive with strong English skills. For these students, the necessity to develop English as quickly as possible is probably their biggest challenge. This is especially true for students for whom a bilingual program is not available. For those students, from the time they step on a school bus or enter a school building, they are bombarded with voices and visuals that may be incomprehensible. How to respond—or even *if* to respond, how to ask for assistance, how to find out where to go, and who to ask for help—are all overwhelming assaults on the mind and the emotions.

Providing a welcoming atmosphere, including bilingual personnel when possible, can make the first few days much less stressful.

In Chapters Four and Five, we will look at how the non-academic needs of all newcomers can be addressed, both within the school day and through collaboration with newcomer families and outside agencies.

Where Are Our Newcomers Coming From?

As you read this next section of the Introduction, add your own notes to this three-column chart based on the newcomers in your school or school district, including preliminary thoughts on the impact these newcomers may have on curriculum design and instruction.

Newcomer groups in my setting	Students with strong educational backgrounds	Students with some educational gaps	Students with severely interrupted schooling
• Home culture and reason for immigration. • Academic or SEL needs. • Impact on curriculum design and instruction			

Another way to look at newcomers is to think about how and why they came to the United States. Just as most of our newcomers fit generally into three main categories of English and academic proficiency, they also fit into three categories of immigrant. The first group are families who come through the visa process. Some, such as those who are granted a visa and ultimately a green card based on family sponsorship and those who win the visa lottery, may eventually obtain permanent resident status. Those on a work visa or student visa are non-immigrants with permission to stay in the United States for work or school. All these families generally plan their move for months or even years, although those on non-immigrant visas generally cannot count on staying in the United States permanently. Most of the children in these families are on par with their peers in literacy, numeracy, and academic content. Even when these children have not been exposed to English, they make progress relatively quickly because they understand school structure and can make the transition more easily to this new language because of their academic and literacy background.

A second group of immigrant students are those who come as refugees. For most of the past 40 years, the United States has been the main country of resettlement, often resettling as many refugees as the rest of the world combined. While the number of refugees entering the United States varies annually due to multiple reasons, our country's dedication to supporting this vulnerable population remains. Many, if not most, of our students who enter as refugees have experienced severe trauma and may need support beyond academics. In addition, the schooling they may have received in refugee camps is often subpar, and a large percentage of children attended school sporadically, if at all, while in camp (UNHCR, 2022).

The third group of students loosely fit into the category of "asylees." These are individuals who are awaiting their political asylum case to be heard and those whose cases have been approved. This also includes families who have been given permission to stay until the situation in their home country improves, a category known as temporary protected status (TPS). TPS is granted by the president based on home country and varies each year. Details on updated TPS countries can be found on the US Citizenship and Immigration Service website (https://www.uscis.gov/humanitarian/temporary-protected-status). Those granted asylum have a path to permanent residency, while those with TPS do not have such a path based on their status. Asylees and individuals with TPS have permission to stay in the United States, and their children have the right to attend school.

> *In fact, any individual of school age (which varies by state) who is living in the United States has the right to attend school according to the 1982 Supreme Court case of Plyler v. Doe. (Plyler v. Doe)*

Political asylum is based on the Geneva Convention. In 1951, the United States was a signatory to the Geneva Convention, which guaranteed the right of anyone to request political asylum in another country. For decades, the US government has permitted individuals to request asylum and a hearing would be scheduled for the case to be heard. However, because of the large number of cases, the hearing was often held several years after the request. This allowed the individual to stay in the country legally until the case was settled. This practice has been under scrutiny and has seen numerous legal and political challenges. The future of political asylum in the United States is unclear, but some form will undoubtedly remain.

One group of individuals especially impacted by the future of political asylum is that of "unaccompanied minors." This term refers to any child, under the age of 18, who comes to the United States without the protection of a parent or guardian. After a short detention, they are either placed in long-term care, foster care, or reunited with friends or family. It is estimated by the Department of Customs and Border Protection that about 100,000 minors arrived in the United States during federal year 2023 (Ventura, 2023). Most of these children requested political asylum, and they may stay in the United States and attend school until their case is completed. A large percentage may eventually face deportation, especially those without legal representation.

The number of individuals presenting themselves at the southern border, a mix of Mexican and Central Americans and individuals from other areas of Latin America, including increasing numbers of Venezuelans, Cubans, Haitians, and even people from Africa and Asia, has overwhelmed the immigration system in recent years (Ward and Batalova, 2023). In addition, at the same time, Afghans and Ukrainians have been arriving in record numbers. Families who would normally be arriving through the typical refugee resettlement system have been pushed to the back of the line. Government resources, including funding and personnel, have been rerouted to provide for these unusual situations. However, regardless of the country of origin of these new arrivals, most are arriving at the school doors with critical academic and social/emotional needs that must be addressed.

Each year, as the political, economic, and climate situation changes around the world, the origin of our recent immigrants will vary, but immigrants will continue to arrive in the United States. Since the founding of our country, the push of global disruption and the pull of the American Dream has brought newcomers to our borders and to our classrooms. While the numbers may fluctuate based on internal and external factors, immigration has not stopped, and there is no reason to believe that anything or anyone will be able to totally curb this phenomenon. It is not the intent of the authors of this book to debate immigration policy; however, as educators we do need to know as much as possible about the backgrounds of our students to best meet their needs. We need to do our part to make sure that the children who are participants in this flow have their educational and civil rights met in our classrooms.

While school personnel may not directly ask students or families about their immigration status, there may be times when services may be impacted by this status. Nurses or counselors especially may find themselves at times needing to talk to parents or students and ask questions in ways that can determine how best to help the child. A nurse may need to find out which health care options the family can access, or the counselor may need to find out if completing a financial aid form can trigger unwanted questions. At all times, it is critical that school personnel assure parents that school employees in the United States are not permitted to discuss a child's immigration status with the government and that such information is always confidential.

What Needs Do Newcomers Bring to Our Classrooms?

We will look at two main areas of need for our newcomers: academic and social/emotional. The two areas are intertwined and often overlap as well as influence each other. For example, poor attendance can be the result of home issues but will also affect a student's ability to be successful in the classroom.

Because all newcomers are entering an unfamiliar school setting, students will need some basic orientation for a few weeks. For students who have had little or no experience with formal schooling, this orientation may take much longer. For elementary students, learning about cooperative learning and classroom movement to work in pairs, triads, or cooperative groups will need to be introduced. Movement within classrooms may be unfamiliar, as students in many global settings sit in rows and are spoken to, with little opportunity to interact with the teacher or their peers. Many schools in the United States rely less on lecture and more on pair or group work and individual activities, which may cause initial discomfort for new arrivals. And most secondary students will also need an introduction to how school "works" in the United States, especially in the areas of transcript evaluation, credits, sports, extracurricular activities, grade point average, etc.

Students whose schooling has been severely interrupted may have major gaps in literacy and numeracy knowledge and skills as well as difficulty in content area subjects, such as science and social studies. Many of our SLIFE also have limited literacy in their home language and, when possible, need heritage language classes to build their first language academic reading and writing skills.

Students who come at high school age often are not familiar with the career and technical opportunities available to them while still in secondary school and can use support to access these programs. They probably will not be aware of the complicated post-secondary application process, including college entrance exams and the Free Application for Federal Student Aid (FAFSA). And finally, they will require information on how to access the many supports available to them both inside the school and in the community.

Please note: Most students who are considering post-secondary education are encouraged to complete a FAFSA application. Students who are undocumented should **not** complete this form and submit it to the government. This is because they are ineligible for the aid provided through the application and submitting the application can trigger questions or problems from the government. Students who are citizens or legal permanent residents with a green card who live in mixed immigration status households (including those with undocumented parents) are eligible for federal aid and should complete the form.

In addition to academic challenges, many of our newcomers have social and emotional issues that impact their education. Some have experienced traumatic events in their lives and may need support to deal with the aftermath. Other students may arrive with physical and emotional health issues that require time and attention. Some older students may need adapted hours to be able to work or because they come with children of their own. Each of these situations requires a program that is flexible and attuned to the needs of the students.

This book will look in depth at each of these situations and offer potential solutions to often complex problems. We hope that within the covers of this book, you will find the information and resources you need to best support your new arrivals.

Self-Study or Group Study Activities

1. Reflect on this introductory chapter in your journal or discuss with your peers. What are your immediate thoughts after reading this information? How does this compare with what you have observed in your own school setting? What are your concerns about this burgeoning population? What do you hope to learn about newcomers from this book?

2. As you begin to explore academic learning and social-emotional learning (SEL) issues for newcomers, what concerns are most critical in working with your newcomers? In the Venn diagram below, or with your own graphic, jot some notes about both academic and social-emotional concerns. Indicate where you think both concerns intersect. Save these notes to revisit after further chapter readings.

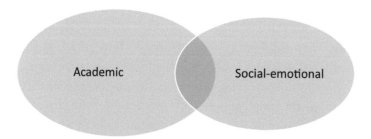

Figure 1: Academic and Social-Emotional Issues for Newcomers

Five Best Practices for Meeting the Academic, Social, and Emotional Needs of Newcomers

Through our research and personal experience, we have created a list of best/most effective practices for serving newly arrived English learners. Each chapter in this book will be an expansion of one of these practices.

> **Best Practice Number One:** Collaborate with school/district professionals to create a program specifically to meet the unique needs of your new arrivals.
>
> In Chapter One, we will look at the various configurations for serving newcomers, from elementary through adults, including specific populations such as SLIFE and students with disabilities.
>
> **Best Practice Number Two:** Provide intensive literacy, numeracy, and content area support, especially for students with interrupted schooling.
>
> Commonly referred by the acronym of SLIFE, students with gaps in their previous schooling need additional time and resources to make up for lost time. Chapter Two offers specific strategies for supporting SLIFE.
>
> **Best Practice Number Three:** Develop the classroom supports necessary for students to achieve academic success.
>
> Chapter Three provides specific strategies and scaffolds to help newcomers build English proficiency, access the curriculum, and demonstrate their new skills.

Best Practice Number Four: Provide supports that address the physical, social, emotional, and educational challenges of newcomers.

Many newcomers enter classrooms with barriers that prevent them from being able to fully concentrate on schoolwork. Chapter Four provides insight into ways to reduce these barriers and build resiliency.

Best Practice Number Five: Work with families and communities to support students outside of the school environment.

Chapter Five describes how the school can work together with the larger community to provide the support that newcomers and their families need during their transition to their new home.

By the end of this text, it is the desire of the authors that school personnel will have a clearer picture of the backgrounds of their new arrivals, will be informed as to which programs and strategies could help their students make the most academic and social-emotional progress, and will strive to discover ways to better integrate their students into the fabric of the school and school system.

CHAPTER ONE

Newcomer Program Designs and Variations

Best Practice Number One: Collaborate with school/district professionals to create a program specifically to meet the unique needs of your new arrivals.

Serving your new arrivals can take many forms, depending on the number of students, their level of previous education, their age, the type of programming allowed in your state or school district, and many other factors. By far, the most common programming is to simply integrate these newcomers in an existing ESL or bilingual program. This works if the number of new arrivals is low or scattered throughout various grade levels and/or the school year. However, if a large influx occurs, or the students need additional support because of interrupted education or unusually high levels of trauma, then the school or district may need to develop a designated newcomer model.

In some schools, this programming may involve keeping these students together for specialized assistance. At the elementary level, students may be clustered in certain classes for pull out or push in instruction and/or placed in a self-contained class for additional support or scheduled to be served by additional ESL/bilingual staff. At the secondary level, students may be placed in a series of classes through the day with trained staff so that students can still get content as well as language instruction. If the numbers are large enough, the students may be placed in a dedicated school wing or even attend a separate school designed to meet their needs. There are additional details on secondary programs later in this chapter.

History of Newcomer Programs

Specifically creating programs for new arrivals is not a new concept. One of the first studies on newcomer programs was conducted by Hedy Chang for California Tomorrow in 1990, more than 30 years ago (now called Californians Together, a non-profit educational organization). She focused on newcomer programs in California, reporting that the first known newcomer program was in San Francisco in 1969. In her report, she stated that "language learning alone is inadequate to ensure newcomer children's success in school. Many newcomers have had little schooling even in their native language or have suffered educational interruptions. They may require adapted or re-designed curricula and help to catch up with their peers" (Chang, 1990, p. 9). This purpose for setting up a newcomer program is just as valid, if not more so, today as in 1990.

Another early study of newcomer programs was published in the following year by Monica Friedlander. She defined newcomer programs as "temporary transitional programs designed to meet the unique needs of newcomer students in the context of a nurturing and supportive education environment" (Friedlander, 1991, p. 2). She describes the function of a newcomer program as a ***temporary stopover***—the equivalent of a cultural and educational shock absorber—for recently arrived immigrant and refugee students. She believed that one of the major benefits of newcomer programs was the fact that they could offer students a comprehensive array of academic and support services tailored to their specific needs in a concentrated and one-stop-shop format.

If the benefits are myriad, why then are newcomer programs still relatively rare? Schools and districts face several challenges in designing and implementing a program for new arrivals. First, knowledge of the best practices for supporting English learners is still not widespread among some administrators, funding and regulations vary greatly from state to state, and the fear of isolating and labeling students prevents districts from serving new arrivals separately from their peers. In addition, civil rights concerns and law indicate that English learners should be able to be integrated into all school programs and social activities in which native English learners participate. So how can these programs meet student needs while not violating their rights? By providing students and their families with informed choice and a plan for exiting when students are ready.

Other potential challenges in creating a newcomer program for English learners include:

- Obtaining district approval and funding for a program that may not be well understood.

- Finding staff that is certified and sensitive to the needs of the students and their families.
- Adapting state and district curriculum to meet the needs of a variety of students.
- Dealing with the accountability requirements of your state and the federal government, including meeting graduation rate requirements because many students come overage, with limited educational backgrounds, and low SES, and expecting students to meet the four-year cohort requirement of many states because of the time needed to build literacy and academic skills, well as English proficiency.

One of the most comprehensive studies of newcomer services was conducted by the Center of Applied Linguistics in two stages, the first part in the 1990s and a follow-up study in the early 2000s. Surveys were sent to school districts across the United States to find out who had specific programming for new arrivals and where these programs were located. Information from the 115 respondents was published in two formats. The first study resulted in a book titled *Creating Access: Language and Academic Programs for Secondary School Newcomers* (2006) in which the data collected by the surveys were compiled and analyzed. The second report, *Helping Newcomers Succeed in Secondary Schools and Beyond*, describes a follow-up study and was published in 2012 by the Center for Applied Linguistics (which is still available on the center's cal.org website as a free downloadable book).

Both studies found that the designs for newcomer programs were as varied as the number of districts responding. Each school district, and at times even different individual schools within a district, was creating a program that worked for their unique situation. Each program design matched the needs of the students being served. Listed below are the major areas that the study found had been considered when planning a newcomer program:

Program Design Considerations

- Grades to be served (elementary, middle, and/or high). Overwhelmingly, most newcomer programs and services are designed for secondary students for two reasons. The gap between student academic performance and skill level and the grade level expectations is the greatest at middle and high school. Also, elementary teachers are better trained to build basic literacy and numeracy skills for new arrivals, and scheduling is more flexible for younger students.

- Course offerings (some schools offered just ESL, others also had bilingual or heritage language classes, and many provided content courses in English and/or in home languages). All newcomer programs had a strong focus on English development, but not all were able to provide home language support. About half of the schools surveyed offered some form of bilingual programming based on the size of the language group being served and the language development options offered in various states. For students who had interrupted schooling, many districts felt it was critical that students build literacy in both the home language and English.

- Length of newcomer programming (only one period, a partial day, a whole day, or only after school). The amount of time available for participation in the program varied based on staffing, busing, and scheduling options.

- Expanded learning opportunities (ELOs) (summer school, Saturday school, or after school options). Additional time to build language skills, focus on content, and prepare for life after secondary school may require students to attend these ELOs. Schools had to be creative to attract student participation by offering transportation and including fun activities such as sports or arts.

- Amount of time students may remain before exiting (one semester, one school year, longer based on progress toward proficiency). Most programs (about 64%) allowed students to stay up to two years depending on when in the school year they enrolled. Some of the programs were whole school programs that allowed students to stay until graduation, and all allowed students to exit when they desired or when they had reached certain exit criteria.

- Curriculum development and material selection. This was a concern for all programs. Finding the appropriate material for simultaneous language and content development for students at the emerging level continues to remain a struggle two decades later.

- Career exploration and internships. These were offered in most of the high school-level programs, and career counseling was available at about a third of the schools.

- Interaction with native speakers. How to ensure this was more of a challenge in separate school programs. The vast majority of the programs were housed within a larger school, and interaction usually occurred in elective classes and at lunch. Creative scheduling was used in other cases to encourage opportunities for students to meet and spend time with native English speakers.

- State assessment requirements. Rules for newcomers varied from state to state and over time. Most states offered at least a short time in which newcomers were exempt from state testing.

- Administration/staff selection and criteria. This also varied across states. Teacher and paraprofessional certification requirements were based on state requirements. The researchers acknowledged the crucial role that administrators make in the creation and daily operation of a newcomer program regardless of size and the difficulty in finding individuals trained in working with new arrivals.

- Content area certification needed for courses. Certification for subjects such as English as a second language (ESL) science, ESL social studies, and ESL mathematics varied depending on state regulations. Some states required that staff have dual certification in their content area and in second language development, but most relied on professional development to train content staff to serve newcomers.

- Professional development/training needed. Most of the programs in the study reported that on-going training was considered a priority, especially for new hires.

- Paraprofessionals (number, language, hiring criteria, placement, training). The use of bilingual personnel to assist in the classroom and elsewhere in the school occurred in about 75% of the programs. Their role in helping students feel welcome and safe cannot be overstated.

- Support staff. Jobs such as secretary, counselor, nurse, social worker, and parent/community liaison are critical. No school can operate without support staff, and this is even more evident in a newcomer program. When possible, schools tried to find bilingual personnel to fill these roles, providing even more role models for students and helping them with the transition to the new school.

See Chapter Four for more details on the various staff roles in a newcomer program.

From our research and school visits, we have found four common program models at the secondary level. (We will discuss low incidence programs and elementary options later in this chapter.) The most common model is simply a class or strand of classes for the new arrivals. This works well if the numbers are low or if students are slowly being added to the existing English language development (ELD) program. No additional personnel are needed beyond the ESL teacher; simply use material appropriate for emergent level students.

Once the numbers reach a certain level, to be determined by the district or the school, many schools move to the school-within-a-school model. This can involve a cluster of classrooms, a wing of the building, or a floor dedicated to the newcomer classes. One obvious advantage to this arrangement is that the issue of transportation, support staff, administration, transition, and integration with native speakers is solved because the students are simply integrated into an existing school. Students can be scheduled into the appropriate classes as needed and transition out much more easily when they are ready.

A third model is rarer but effective when newcomers are scattered across several buildings in a larger district. The use of a separate site to house students, often for part of the day or for certain days of the week, was used in about 15% of the schools in the Short and Boyson (2012) study referenced above. Some of these served both middle and high school students, with one group coming in the morning and the other group in the afternoon. This configuration also encourages students to feel more a part of their home school and eases the transition when the newcomer program is complete. This type of programming usually focuses on language development and possibly basic math or a course such as technology or art. When the students return to their home school, they can take their science or social studies and elective courses.

The final type of newcomer program, the whole school model, was the least common (only about 10%), but over 60% of the students attended this style of programming because the programs were larger, and students stayed for more than one year. A few of these programs were offered at both middle and high school while others concentrated on one level. Several of the schools using this model have joined together for curriculum development and training purposes into the Internationals Network. This network began in New York City in 2004 and now contains about 30 schools in 12 school districts from the east coast to California. In the whole school model, students can remain in the school until graduation if they choose. Most

Figure 2: Critical Components of a Newcomer Program

programs offer both English development and bilingual programming when appropriate based on numbers, as well as classes in whatever courses are needed for graduation.

Each school and school district should consider its resources, the numbers and needs of its particular student population, and state policies to determine which of these programs would be most appropriate for its newcomers.

Critical Components of a Newcomer Program

Whether a program design is extensive or basic, there are some components that must be included to ensure that newcomer needs are being met:

- an orientation to the school system regulations and expectations for all new arrivals,
- English language development for students without English proficiency,
- first language development, when possible,
- literacy and numeracy development for students with interrupted schooling,
- a transition plan for movement out of the newcomer program, and
- information on graduation requirements and post-secondary options for secondary students.

School orientation is a valuable component of any newcomer program. It can give students time to adjust to new school norms and a safe place to provide training in and opportunities to practice appropriate school behavior. It can also give students time to familiarize themselves with the classroom dynamics of US schools, since some students tend to see the relaxed nature of a typical US classroom as the equivalent of no rules. For students who may have been out of school for a long period of time, or who may never have been in a formal school setting, the idea of sitting for hours in a classroom is a difficult adjustment. A newcomer classroom can help students adjust to spending extended periods of time on academic tasks, such as reading or writing. For students who have moved frequently, or who have left family and friends behind, this new setting can help them overcome the difficulty of making friends. And finally, it can help students and families to realize the value of consistent attendance and the role of high school graduation in Western society.

Enrollment centers are often the first contact that families have with a school district. In addition to English language screening and placement services, these centers may provide an assessment of the student's native language proficiency and many times may also offer an assessment of a student's math skills as well as assistance with scheduling (especially at the middle and high school level). Newcomer programs or enrollment centers may also provide "wrap-around services," such as a health clinic for screening and vaccinations, counseling services, and connections to social services for the students and their families. These types of non-academic services are often available in the languages of the family. Chapter Four is dedicated to additional information on these types of services and how they can provide valuable support to new arrivals.

Whether the enrollment occurs in a district center or at the school level, there are a few things that should be kept in mind. First, any child living in the United States may legally attend public schools if they meet the age requirements of the state. Enrollment is not based on immigration status of the child or the parents, based on the US Supreme Court decision Plyler v. Doe, 1982. In fact, schools are prohibited from even asking for any documents that would reveal the immigration status of the child. It is permissible to ask for documents that show the student's age, address (to make sure they live in the district in which they are enrolling), and guardianship.

The district is also required to determine if the child needs language assistance and to offer language services if needed. This begins with a home language survey, some version of which is required in each state. If the parents indicate that there is a language other than English present in the home, then an assessment must be given to determine the student's English language proficiency. Most states use the WIDA screener, others use a screener developed for ELPA21 states, and some states have created their own screener. If the screener reveals that the student needs English language services, services must be offered. And even if the parent refuses to accept service, the school must still find a way to provide English services without a formal program.

Finally, schools should keep in mind that some newcomers arrive in their new school, and possibly in their new country, without a permanent home. The family may be temporarily living with friends or family, they may have been placed in temporary housing by an agency, or the child may have arrived alone and is staying wherever they can find shelter. In all of these cases, the child is considered homeless, and the school needs to consider the requirements of the McKinney-Vento Homeless Assistance Act. This act states that a child must be allowed to enroll in the nearest school until permanent housing is found. The McKinney-Vento Act requires schools to enroll students experiencing homelessness immediately, even if the student is unable to provide documents that are typically required for enrollment, such as previous academic records, records of immunization and other required health records, proof of residency, or other documentation (McKinney-Vento Homeless Assistance Act, 2015).

Equally important to the decision for how to place a student into a newcomer program is a plan for the transition out of the newcomer program. Many districts simply put a time limit on the program, and a student exits the program at the end of a semester or a year. Other programs use exit criteria based on English proficiency. Still others will gradually transition the student into sheltered or mainstream classes in the same building when the student is ready. Many programs have a transition team to periodically review each student and determine any changes required in student services. If the newcomer program is housed in a separate site, it is critical that the students are able visit the new location and familiarize themselves with their future placement. While there is no one correct or best transition plan, it is important that the student and the family know *how* the decision will be made and *when*. And of course, the family always must have the right and the power to deny any services about which they feel uncomfortable.

Low Incidence Programs

The term "low incidence" refers to schools and school districts that have small numbers of multilingual learners across multiple grade levels.

Low incidence numbers of multilingual learners can be described as including, but not limited to, the following:

- Small numbers of learners of a particular language group spread out over multiple grades. They may not fit in a traditional bilingual program model because their language is different from the other members of the program, or their language is new to the district and there are no certified teachers who speak their language.

- Small numbers of learners, in different grades and/or different language and culture groups. There are no significant numbers in any language group or any grade levels/level clusters to form an ESL grade level and/or a bilingual grade level program.

- A few secondary learners in different grades and different language and culture groups, often with different native-language educational experiences and taking different courses.

Each of these scenarios presents a scheduling and instructional dilemma for the English language educator. In elementary settings, when teachers have small numbers, scattered across multiple grades, such as one first grader, two second graders, two third graders, three fourth graders, and two fifth graders, they struggle with how best to serve the students. And the situation is compounded when, as described in the second bullet above, these students are from different language and culture groups.

Building a program in this situation is best accomplished by combining grade level numbers to form language and content learning groups. For example, first and second grade students can be taught together, and grades 3-5 can be taught together. Another consideration is to keep kindergarten or first grade as a single-grade group for instruction focused on basic literacy skills, survival language, school vocabulary, and oral language activities, including reading aloud. Then grades 2-3 could be taught together, and grades 4-5 can be taught together.

For both grade clusters, grades 2-3 and grades 4-5, instruction should be built around introducing language through content thematically. Since in most elementary schools there are several topics that are consistently taught at similar grade levels, as the ESL teacher you can focus on an "umbrella" topic or theme that would touch on content covered in both grades. For example, the theme of "habitats" or "communities" (grades 2-3) and "our planet, the Earth" or "the American Revolution" (grades 4-5) could be explored thematically. As you explore these themes, you can introduce academic vocabulary; oral language production; reading, including the use of picture books for the content; and writing with support. Expanding on any one of these topics takes you beyond the initial lessons. For example, "our planet, the Earth" can expand into "earthquakes and natural disasters" and beyond into "exploring the solar system."

For secondary low incidence populations, the situation is more complicated and requires a schedule for small-group or one-on-one tutorial sessions by grade level, including a focus not only on social language but also on academic language learning for key subjects. When possible, periodic observations by the ESL teacher or paraprofessional in the content classes, along with small group support, would help with building an understanding of content. Creating a schedule that combines daily English lessons with the ESL teacher with two to three days a week of scheduled "push ins" to assist with content learning would be ideal. This requires cooperation and communication with the content teachers as well as a time in the content classroom when all students, not only the English learners, can be working in small groups. In larger middle and high schools, scheduling the new arrivals with a limited number of teachers can allow for co-planning and targeted support. When students are scattered across the school, this becomes an overwhelming and nearly impossible task.

Elementary Programs

Elementary ESL programs require careful consideration of the population of newcomers at each grade level and/or grade band. In some programs, if there are a significant number of newcomers, there can be a **self-contained class** with mixed grade levels, staffed by two teachers, a certified ESL or bilingual teacher and a certified elementary teacher team, teaching both language and content. Another possible scenario would be to have a **partial-day newcomer grade-level class** for language development and the remainder of the day for reading, writing, and content instruction by a grade-level elementary teacher.

ESL and/or bilingual teachers can also push into a grade K-5 class and **co-teach language and content**. The ESL and/or bilingual teacher can be a co-teacher in several K-5 classrooms, pushing in to co-teach. With a smaller number of newcomers, a school can also use **clustering**, which is selecting one or two teachers per grade level to each have a small group of newcomers. This allows the ESL or bilingual teacher to focus on a smaller number of teachers for co-teaching and planning, rather than an entire grade level. Another service model for elementary newcomers is **looping,** which means that the same elementary teacher teaches the same group of learners for two grades, such as grades 2 and 3 and the same ESL/bilingual teacher services that same group of students for two years. Collaborating and co-planning are key for looping, as well as differentiating instruction for newcomer needs, based on team decisions (Yzquierdo, 2017, p. 157).

> **Suggested materials for elementary newcomer classes**: literacy kits for teaching phonemic awareness and phonics; vocabulary flashcards with visuals, alphabet strips, picture books such as alphabet books, basic concept books, non-fiction titles for content, pattern books, and anchor charts of basic vocabulary.

Vignette: Newcomer classes by grade bands (K, 1, 2-3, 4-5 or K, 1-2, 3-5) were mentioned earlier in the information on low incidence and often work well for groups of learners. We observed an ESL teacher working with her elementary class of grades 3 and 4 newcomers. She was conducting a lesson on body parts, with a focus on doctor visits. She provided medical instruments to discuss the names of each instrument and what each was used for. One focus of the lesson was to help alleviate the fear of going to the doctor. The teacher used a book with pictures of body parts, as well as the realia (objects from everyday life, in this case the group of medical instruments the students could touch and talk about) and sentence stems, to provide students opportunities to practice conversations. For example, "Doctor, my _____ hurts." Her exit ticket for the day was having the students practice different phrases, such as: "I need a translator please. I don't speak English" (Jury, 2023).

Secondary Programs

The most frequently offered newcomer programs are those designed for secondary students. Many of these students have an interrupted or incomplete education. The US Department of Education and the US Department of Justice, interpreting the mandates of civil rights laws and requirements, have made it clear that regardless of these educational gaps, students should be placed in age-appropriate grade placement and specially designed curricula should be provided to bridge the gaps resulting from interrupted or incomplete education.

In a landmark Dear Colleague Letter for English Learners issued in January 2015 to all school superintendents in the United States, the US Department of Education Office for Civil Rights and the US Department of Justice, Civil

Rights Division, jointly instruct that such students need to be given age-appropriate instruction. Schools have the responsibility of designing academic programs for these students in such a way that gaps in education are filled as quickly as possible. With specific reference to students with interrupted formal education, the Dear Colleague Letter recognizes that districts must provide appropriately specialized programs to meet the needs of these students. The departments state they would not consider these specialized programs to be inappropriate or a violation of federal civil rights law "where the program is age-appropriate" (Dear Colleague Letter, 2015, footnote 50).

> School districts…should place EL students in age-appropriate grade levels so that they can have meaningful access to their grade-appropriate curricula and an equal opportunity to graduate. (p. 18)

The Dear Colleague Letter also repeatedly emphasizes there must be a clear and timely pathway to graduation, citing in part Castañeda v. Pickard, 1981:

> For an EL program to be reasonable calculated to ensure that EL students attain equal participation in the standard instructional program within a reasonable length of time, if an EL student enters the ninth grade with beginner-level English proficiency, the school district should offer EL services that would enable him/her to earn a regular high-school diploma in four years. In addition, EL students in high school, like their never-EL peers, should have the opportunity to be competitive in meeting college entrance requirements. For example, a school district should ensure that there are no structural barriers within the design of the academic program that would prevent EL students who enter ninth grade with limited English proficiency from graduating on time with the prerequisites to enter college. (pp. 19–20)

It is fully recognized that this is not a simple task and that it requires creativity and flexibility on the part of a school district. But, at the same time, this is not an insurmountable task, and many school districts successfully manage the challenge. In addition to the federal legal requirements for age-appropriate education, there are individual states that have state requirements for such age-appropriate curriculum and placement as well.

The key here, as reflected in the Dear Colleague Letter, is to ensure a timely path to high school graduation. Further, it is commonly accepted that, in education, placement with same-age peers is the most desirable placement and that deviation from that principle often leads to a psychosocial impact on a student and could lead to an increased likelihood of a dropout from school.

In the process of placement of these students and development of specialized programs for them, it is very important that school districts take care to examine transcripts or available records provided by these students and, in the absence of such transcripts or complete records, it is important that districts reconstruct actual course offerings completed by students in their home countries through interviews with the students and their parents. There have been multiple guides developed that establish the equivalency of courses in other countries to those in the United States.

It is very important to the student that equivalencies are determined to the extent possible. A common example of the challenge of course equivalencies is that in many countries, math and science are not divided into separate topics, such as algebra and geometry, or chemistry and biology, but just called "maths" or "sciences." Each year, the student takes a mixture of different types of math and science, combined under the generic title. Districts must determine how they will parse out these subjects on the transcripts to match the courses offered in their state.

In summary, it is our recommendation that counselors or administrators who are given the task of evaluating transcripts work as closely as possible with students and their families to determine what courses have already been taken to prevent students from having to repeat courses. Some districts have created placement exams or use end-of-course exams to allow students to show proficiency and prevent them from having to retake courses. The challenge may be in finding or translating assessments into the native language. There is also the issue that, even if a student can show academic proficiency in a course, they may not yet have the English proficiency to be successful in the next higher course, especially if it is language intense, such as geometry. There is no good answer, and each district or school needs to make these determinations on an individual basis with consideration of staff, resources, student skill, and age-appropriate placement.

It is also extremely important for educators planning curriculum for students from other countries, and particularly for those students with interrupted or incomplete educations, to understand that the curriculum in many countries often surpasses that offered in US K-12 schools. For example, if a student completes high school in Mexico, they generally have had the equivalent of two years of post-secondary instruction in the United States. In those situations, a student from Mexico who is two years shy of a full high school degree in Mexico may have what is the equivalent of a full US high school curriculum, with the obvious exception of some US or state history requirements or similar courses.

Further, school districts should strongly consider giving credit for fluency in other languages besides English to take the place of language course requirements for graduation. This approach also provides an opportunity for a district to fashion additional instruction time to replace missed coursework in the slots where scheduling for language courses would otherwise be required. In addition, most states now offer the **Seal of Biliteracy** for students who demonstrate proficiency in English and in a second language. Some states are using this seal as one step to graduation, and some universities are using the seal to provide college credit for a foreign language. Check with your state to see what benefits this seal can offer for your students.

Programming for Older Teens

The issue of serving students who come in their late teen years is a complicated one. In most states, students are allowed to attend public school until a certain age, usually 21 or 22. However, schools and districts are reluctant to enroll a student who may not be able to complete their high school requirements by that cutoff date or who may possibly need more than the traditional four years, which is the typical time allotted for districts to graduate students. In states that have school accountability report cards or other accountability measures to show district strengths and weaknesses, districts may discourage or even refuse to enroll students who would negatively impact their scores.

One district in Pennsylvania was recently involved in a lawsuit because they placed their overage enrollees in a charter school rather than allow them to enter the district high school, and a federal judge ruled that the district had violated the students' civil right to an equal education (see *The School I Deserve* by Jo Napolitano, 2021, for more details on this case). Despite this ruling, it is not unusual for districts to actively discourage overage students from enrolling and often steer them to adult programs instead. It is our belief that the students and their families should be given sufficient information about their alternatives to make the decision themselves on the best placement that matches their future plans.

Programs for Students with Limited or Interrupted Formal Education (SLIFE or SIFE)

Many newcomer programs have as their initial impetus a desire to serve students with significant gaps in their schooling. These are often the individuals for whom a traditional language program is not sufficient. These students are often described using the acronyms of SIFE (students with interrupted formal education) or SLIFE (students with limited or interrupted formal education). The term SIFE was first used in New York City in the 1990s and is still used in many states. The acronym SLIFE was coined by Andrea DeCapua and her fellow authors, William Smathers and Lixing Frank Tang, in their book *Meeting the Needs of Students with Limited or Interrupted Education* (2009). The letter *L* was added to the older acronym to indicate that some of the students in this category have more than "interrupted" schooling; they may have had extremely limited schooling or even no previous formal education.

There have been very few studies conducted on this subgroup. One team of researchers, Klein and Martohardjono, conducted three studies on this population between 2006 and 2015. They found that the average SIFE in New York City was entering grade 9 with a reading level more than four years below grade level, with some students having no previous exposure to print (Klein & Montahardjono, 2010). Most students in the study had a fifth grade academic vocabulary and a reading comprehension level of grade 3 in their home language. "The research also showed that these SIFE displayed age-appropriate cognitive and native language development; it was in English literacy, academic language and content knowledge that students had fallen behind" (Auslander, 2019, p. 3). The authors of these studies recommended that a program be developed to provide these SIFE with an extra year of high school to help them make the transition from their current skill level to that which would be required by typical high school courses. The Internationals Network of newcomer schools (mentioned earlier in this chapter) has worked to create coursework and curriculum to build literacy and numeracy skills for SIFE that may be used in a transition year when SIFE first enter high school, or which may be used in grade 9 to build basic skills needed for traditional high school courses.

In a 2019 book about newcomer programs in New York City, Lisa Auslander (the project director of the Bridges to Academic Success program at CUNY) stated that "SIFE are a unique population of students. In addition to low literacy levels in their home language, many also struggle with a host of social, emotional, and/or economic difficulties, frequently in relation to the experience of immigrant or refugee status…As a result of these difficulties, SIFE need targeted, age-appropriate curricula and materials for learning to read and write in English, along with specific attention to their social and emotional needs." She went on to say that "There is evidence that the most successful academic programs for SIFE involve culturally responsive teaching, require an understanding of the students and their culture, and use scaffolded educational materials that meet the students at their current level"

(Auslander, 2019, p. 7). This matches the statement in the US Department of Education *Newcomer Toolkit* that "EL services and programs must be educationally sound in theory and effective in practice" (Chapter Two, p. 1).

Vignette: Bridges to Academic Success, a project of the City University of New York (CUNY) serves secondary newcomers, generally grades 6-10, many of whom come to this country as SIFE, which impacts the kinds of resources they need to be successful. In addition to recognizing student needs, this program uses an assets-based model to help leverage the strengths of students based on their interests and life experiences. Bridges to Academic Success curricular programs are designed to serve as part of a multi-tiered systems of support (MTSS) approach to accelerate newcomer acquisition of academic language and literacy skills, while leveraging and encouraging the development of social-emotional learning.

Note: Chapter Two will provide specific strategies and suggestions for building literacy and numeracy skills for English learners, with a focus on students with interrupted schooling, and Chapter Four will discuss how the MTSS process can be implemented with newcomers.

Newcomers with Disabilities

Often school districts either over-classify or under-classify students as learning disabled. This situation is compounded with respect to identification of English learners. Those districts that over-classify often consider language development as a disabling condition. In situations where English learners are under-classified, school districts often mistakenly believe that English language development should come before classification of a multilingual learner as learning disabled. Neither is the correct approach. "To qualify for special education services, a student must have one of the identified disabilities under IDEA [Individuals with Disabilities Education Act], and that disability must adversely affect his or her educational performance" and academic learning (Yzquierdo, 2017, p. 36). For multilingual learners to be classified under IDEA, the learner must demonstrate that the disability exists in *all* the languages spoken. In other words, the disability makes it difficult for the multilingual learner to learn in any language, whether English or their native language/languages.

It is important to understand that students who are identified as learning disabled qualify for both special education services for academic needs and ESL and/or bilingual education for second language development. Assessment for special education should be conducted in the learner's stronger/strongest language, which is usually the first or native language.

Parent meetings to discuss placement and the educational plan should be conducted in the parents' native language or with a qualified interpreter, a person who has trained to interpret highly confidential information. A family friend, a child from the family, a neighbor, or anyone else with a personal connection to the family should not be used as they will not understand the complexities of the process. The individual educational plan (IEP) should also be available for parents to read in their native language or be explained orally if necessary. All efforts should be made to help a family understand the educational plan for their child and that there will be periodic meetings to report on their child's progress. While it may be difficult to determine when a newcomer qualifies for special services, it is critical that students receive all supports they need as soon as possible. Parents should also be informed that a special education program has goals and exit criteria for their learner and enrollment does not mean that a student will be a special needs learner indefinitely. Placement is reviewed annually for both special education and English language services. (See Chapter Four for additional information on serving dual-identified newcomers.)

Newcomers Who Are Gifted and/or Talented

One area in which English learners in general, not just newcomers, are woefully under-identified is in the arena of gifted and/or talented (GT) placement and service. One of the major causes of this discrepancy is the challenge of accurately identifying who qualifies for GT services. The 2023 revised US Department of Education *Newcomer Toolkit* states: "When LEAs [local education agencies/local school districts] lack culturally, developmentally, and linguistically appropriate assessments for MLs [multilingual learners], it makes accurate determinations of gifted and talented newcomer students difficult" (2023, p. 28).

All learners, including newcomers and SLIFE, must be permitted to participate in their schools' gifted and talented programs if they qualify. Giftedness is defined by the National Association for Gifted Children (NAGC) as: "students with gifts and talents who perform—or have the capability to perform—at higher levels compared to others of the same age, experience, and environment in one or more domains." The NAGC indicates in its position paper that there are five key elements that must be addressed to "ensure equitable identification and comprehensive services." Among these is the inclusion of students from "all racial, ethnic, and cultural populations" (National Association for Gifted Children, 2019).

Gifted identification of newcomers and/or SLIFE learners may require other methods instead of pencil and paper tests or tasks. These may include performance activities, including demonstration of skills in science, technology, engineering, and/or the arts (music, drawing, painting, etc.). Accommodations may be necessary for language needs, such as translation of directions into native language, visuals, and modeling, and/or a classroom aide or a volunteer who speaks the native language of the learner. As an alternative to potentially biased assessments, some districts are asking for teacher recommendation, but this requires that the teacher be familiar with the criteria for gifted placement, be able to note giftedness present in a newcomer's performance, and would obviously be impacted by teacher judgement.

> Federal civil rights law requires that English learners be given the same access to all school programs and activities that native English speakers are given, including access to gifted services.

Due to these placement issues, some districts choose to wait until students have a stronger use of the English language before placement based on traditional assessments, a choice that can prevent students from getting the placement they need. A better way is when schools focus on other avenues of placement, such as math achievement, artistic talent, or musical ability. An excellent overview and set of recommendations can be found in Chapter 4 of the *Newcomer Toolkit*, "Serving Gifted English Learners" (2023, pp. 13–14). Additionally, the NAGC, based in Washington, DC, provides resources and support for gifted programming for English learners. It indicates on its website (nagc.org) their focus in the position paper "Identifying and Serving Culturally and Linguistically Diverse Gifted Learners."

Newcomer Programs for Adults

Adult English learners, like children, come to their new country with educational and life experiences that range from working as preliterate subsistence farmers to professionals with advanced degrees. Programming to meet their needs must be just as diverse. Most adults who come with limited educational backgrounds usually come either as refugees who were forced from their homes due to war or natural disasters or as individuals looking for relief from economic or political distress. They will often need extensive support just to learn to function in a world that demands functional literacy for survival. Oral English is a start, but job safety and life skills require written skills as well. Some level of English is required to obtain a driver's license, rent an apartment, go to medical visits, and apply for and keep even the most basic jobs. These are often referred to as "soft skills" and are taught in many adult education programs. The top five soft skills areas in adult education are: civics education, digital literacy, financial literacy, health literacy, and workforce preparation. Some EL adults are fortunate enough to find employment working with and/or for other members of their language and culture group, but to move beyond these jobs, a higher level of English proficiency will be required.

Most adult immigrants have at least a basic level of literacy in their home language, and many are very well educated and may have held positions of prestige and power in their home country. For most of these individuals, English classes will range from introductory life skills to the academic literacy needed for graduate school or professional careers. Many internationally trained professionals will need assistance with transferring their skills and certificates into the licensing requirements of their new state or country.

To support English language development and workplace preparation, the federal government created the Integrated English Literacy and Civics Education program (IELCE). This program is "intended to promote economic, linguistic, and civic integration by helping adult immigrants and adult English learners (ELs) 'achieve competency in the English language and acquire the basic and more advanced skills needed to function effectively as parents, workers, and citizens.'" Hofstetter and Cherewka, 2022, quoting WIOA legislation, section 2(1)). The plan behind this program was to create specific training programs that combined English development in conjunction and simultaneously with training in specific job skills. One of the driving forces behind this program was a desire to help immigrants with high skill levels transition to the workforce in the United States. The US Department of Education, Office of Career, Technical, and Adult Education has a website that lists a plethora of resources for supporting programs for adults (lincs.ed.gov).

Programming for adults can be found in such disparate locations as church basements, public libraries, K-12 schools with evening programs, and community college or university halls. The type of programming is often tied to the age of the English learner, who may have aged out of inclusion in a K-12 school, and the immigration background of the student (because of funding):

- Refugee adults qualify for English, employment, and citizenship classes, which vary in length by state. The federal government guarantees eight months of financial support, in addition to education provided through the Workforce Innovation and Opportunity Act of 2014 (WIOA).

- Individuals who do not qualify for government-supported education, because of economic or immigration status, often rely on community or faith-based organizations.
- School districts often provide English classes for the community at no cost, especially for the parents of children enrolled in their schools.
- Employers may provide job-related training.
- Community colleges and universities offer courses to prepare adults for academic courses, usually for a fee. Some community colleges partner with government programs to provide free classes in English, job training, and citizenship.

The US Department of Education Newcomer Toolkit

Whether you are creating a new program or revising an existing program, the US Department of Education has developed the *Newcomer Toolkit* to help schools and school districts to create services and programs for K-12 newcomers that meet federal guidelines and support the academic achievement of this population of students. The Toolkit contains practical suggestions for welcoming students and their families and for how to best meet their academic and non-academic needs.

The Toolkit also contains a list of "Key Elements of High-Quality Educational Programs for Newcomers" (Chapter 3, pg. 4) that the US Department of Education sees as critical to serving new arrivals:

- A clear mission of excellence in the education of newcomers that values the positive contributions to the school and community that newcomers bring.
- Rich learning opportunities for newcomers that are rigorous and include grade-level content and literacy learning in English and newcomers' home language whenever possible.
- Agreed-upon educational pathways for students that promote coherence across grade levels or school settings.
- Schools that directly support students' education and socio-emotional well-being, agency, and autonomy.

- Regular check-ins with students and concerted efforts to connect families with needed services.
- A program with an asset orientation that values newcomers' home languages, cultures, families, and experiences.
- Educators and staff who focus on continuous improvement of the core academic program with the goal of integrating rigorous academic and language learning to nurture and ripen newcomer students' potential.

These key elements will be expanded upon in Chapters Two and Three, which will offer information and suggestions for serving and supporting the academic needs of newcomer English learners. The focus of Chapter Two will be how to build the literacy and numeracy skills of students who have gaps in their educational experience, while Chapter Three will provide specific classroom strategies for welcoming new arrivals and preparing them for success in content classrooms.

Self-Study or Group Study Activities

1. Several court cases and laws are referenced in this chapter (Plyler v. Doe, the McKinney-Vento Act, the Castañeda v. Pickard decision, the Individuals with Disabilities Education Act (IDEA), and the Dear Colleague Letter regarding English Learners. Discuss with your colleagues how these cases and laws impact your program and how you can use them to advocate for additional services for your newcomers.

2. Brainstorm the components of an orientation program that would fit your setting. Questions to consider: What could the orientation include? Who would be the key personnel involved? Would you include student ambassadors? What could be their role in a school orientation program? How would/could you incorporate native language, if possible? Use the table below or a graphic organizer of your own choosing.

Table 1: Components of an Orientation Program

Orientation Program Components	Key Personnel for Each Component	Roles and Responsibilities	Native Language or Other Supports
			.

3. If you are working with adult learners, what might you want to include in your program for teaching each of these soft skills? This is particularly important for an overage English Learner who is not able to enter a K-12 program, who will need both soft skills instruction as well as English Language instruction in reading, writing, and mathematics, leading to a graduate equivalency degree or general education diploma (GED).

Table 2: Soft Skills for Adult Newcomers

Soft Skill	Potential Curriculum Topics for Adults
Civics Education	
Digital Literacy	
Financial Literacy	
Health Literacy	
Workforce Preparation	

CHAPTER TWO

Academic Supports for Newcomers

Best Practice Number Two: Provide intensive literacy, numeracy, and content area support, especially for students with interrupted schooling.

Literacy Development for Newcomers

Literacy development for newcomers should involve building the reading and writing skills in both the home language and English, especially for students who are below grade level in these areas. However, where to start and how best to teach these critical skills is unclear, especially for individuals who enter beyond grade 3. This is when the focus of *learning to read* becomes instead *reading to learn*. Teachers assume that students already have a basic level of literacy and increasingly use textbooks for students to obtain classroom information for themselves, and most secondary teachers have never been trained to teach basic reading skills. For these students, reading instruction could be considered a Tier 2 intervention because it is a special program beyond typical classroom level instruction and should be implemented in a small group. How to work this into the school day is a question that must be answered by each program, but simply placing these students in regular ESL classes will not provide the extra support and foundational skills that they need.

> Research is clear that literacy skills in the home language directly transfer to learning to read and write in a new language. (August & Hakuta, 1997; Bialystok, 2002)

Listed below are the components of a reading program that must somehow be included in literacy instruction, regardless of the age of the student. This list is a composite taken from three major research projects on reading: The National Reading Panel (NICHHD, 2000), the National Literacy Panel on Language-Minority Children and Youth (August & Shanahan, 2006), and the National Committee on Effective Literacy (Escamilla, Olsen & Slavick, 2022).

Critical Components of a Literacy Program for Newcomers

Phonemic Awareness

Phonemic awareness is the knowledge of the sounds of a language. Although English has 26 letters in its alphabet, there are 44 sounds, most of which are distinct vowel sounds. Children learn the sounds of their home language from birth and do not generally need to have them taught. In typical preschool and primary classrooms, teachers concentrate on distinguishing these sounds, manipulating them with activities such as blending sounds to make words, changing the beginning (onset) and final (rhyme) sounds to create new words, and blending sounds. English learners need these activities as well, but often they are working with some unfamiliar sounds or at least with unfamiliar words. And for many English learners, they may be learning these new sounds and words beyond the typical early years. Research has also shown that after puberty, there are some sounds that people learning a new language cannot distinguish because they are not familiar sounds in their home language. It is possible to learn these new sounds, but it takes much more time and concentrated effort. Many experts in second language reading stress that learning to hear and speak English is critical to being able to read it, because phonemic awareness requires the ability to hear the sounds of the language, at least in your head.

Literacy Connections for the Middle School and High School Newcomer

Phonemic awareness for this learner should include connecting to both social and academic language.

Social words and sounds: Focus on conversational words such as "they" and "say" (looking at the sounds of rhyming words) and onset sounds such as those found in "this," "there," "they," "then," and "dress," "drum," "drink." Teachers can create picture cards to teach meaning at the same time as pronunciation.

Academic words and sounds: Consider the geography topic of landforms. The vocabulary would include "mountain," "valley," "river," "canyon," "plains." Teaching the sounds for each would include the initial consonant; the blend, whether at the beginning or end ("pl," "er"); and the sounds of the vowels (first and final or the blend "ai"). Simultaneously, students should also be learning the definition and use of the word.

Letter Knowledge/Alphabetics

Learning the alphabet is one of the first steps in learning English. Knowing which letters are consonants and which are vowels and knowing the sounds of each is part of phonemic awareness. Most primary programs have a specific sequence of learning the vowel sounds, since these sounds are the ones that give students the greatest difficulty. A quick internet search will provide numerous lists of phonemic scope and sequence charts. With older newcomers, especially those with some familiarity with literacy in their home language and those who use the Roman alphabet, you may choose to start with the alphabet names and sounds and some common sight words rather than the typical phonemic awareness used with younger students. Those sounds still need to be covered, but they can be blended into the reading program in a logical sequence while the students are learning basic oral and written English.

Literacy Connections for the Middle School and High School Newcomer
Introducing the alphabet names and sounds in common social language for middle and high school newcomers could look something like this: Look first at an online picture dictionary with sound/pronunciation capability; in addition, consider English/Spanish cognates for Tier 1 (everyday vocabulary) words to connect Tier 1 learning for newcomers. Add visuals and pronunciation guidance, such as using an online English dictionary with sound.

For content vocabulary, create an A-Z graphic to introduce content words for the newcomer. A good way to do this is to use a topic typically taught in middle or high school, such as space. Remember to include visuals and picture books to connect the terms in an alphabet box; note that certain words have multiple meanings in other content domains or social language (e.g., black, half, total, new, inner, falling), and clearly explain both uses.

Table 3: A-Z Vocabulary List

astronaut astronomy	black hole	comet crater	dwarf star	Earth eclipse	falling star
galaxy gravity	half moon	inner planets	Jupiter	Kuiper belt	lens light years
Mars Mercury meteor Milky Way	new moon north star	observatory orbit outer planets	planet Pluto probe	quarter moon	rings rocket
Saturn solar system star sunspot	telescope total eclipse	universe Uranus	vacuum Venus	white dwarf white giant	x-rays yellow dwarf zenith

Phonics, Decoding, Word Work

Phonics is placing the sounds of a language into the written form. Children traditionally first learn to write their name, simple words in forms such as consonant-vowel-consonant (CVC), and everyday objects needed for school life, and then build their written repertoire as they develop early literacy. For newcomers who may be 10 or 13 or 17, we must move much faster. Students must learn to develop their reading and writing skills as quickly as possible to survive in a literate environment. Programs that help individuals build basic phonics skills may take time, but the extra time will pay great benefits in the long run. Phonemic awareness and phonics skills practice connected to learning academic language are also important for the older learner, who needs to learn a significant amount of vocabulary for academic content in middle and high school.

Literacy Connections for the Middle School and High School Newcomer
Social language should include CVC words, such as "bat," "cat," "dot," "got," etc., and then move into compound words, such as "sidewalk," "notebook," "rainbow," "goldfish," "passport," etc., breaking apart each for individual meanings and meaning differences as a compound word.

For academic language: Explore decoding words and determining meaning based on prefixes and/or suffixes. Decoding content words helps to determine meaning in addition to pronunciation. For example, teach words such as "astronomy" using the prefix "astro" (meaning "star") plus the root word "onomy" (meaning "study of"), or "telescope" with the prefix "tele" (meaning "at a distance" or "over a distance") plus "scope" (meaning "instrument for viewing"). This type of word work helps students eventually decipher new words independently,

Concepts of Print

There are certain concepts of print that are part of emerging literacy instruction: directionality, letter and word spacing, punctuality and paragraphing, visual and text pairing, etc. For individuals who come without home language literacy, this must be specifically taught. Fortunately, most newcomers have developed these basic print concepts in their home language and can easily transfer this knowledge to English. Even speakers of languages that are read right to left or top to bottom can master these basic concepts quickly.

Literacy Connections for the Middle School and High School Newcomer
Concepts of print for the middle and high school newcomer can include schedules, such as bus, sports, or class schedules; then maps and posters for events and activities; as well as book jackets, supermarket flyers, catalogues, and direction sheets for assembling something. With each of these, lessons can include important order of operation language, directions, sequencing, and life skills. Learning new vocabulary, practicing pronunciation, and pointing out phonics details (blends, long and short vowels, silent letters, etc.) are connected to concepts of print for the older newcomer.

Knowledge of Text Structure

Students need to be introduced to and become familiar with the two main types of text structure: narrative and non-fiction. Narrative text comes in various genres, each of which has its own format and style, including plotline components and order of information. Newcomers should be introduced to short stories, picture and chapter books, graphic novels, and stories told through non-print media. Non-fiction texts, especially those with visuals, are also perfect for newcomers. Topics such as biographies, science, and social studies help newcomers combine reading development with vocabulary and content knowledge.

Literacy Connections for the Middle School and High School Newcomer: Narrative Text

It is important for students in middle and high school to understand the text structure of narrative text and how it works to develop characters, plot, and resolution. There are various ways to teach and for students to understand narrative text. The first level is with a graphic organizer that divides the aspects of text into meaningful divisions.

Table 4: Plot Chart

Fill in this chart with the basic information from a narrative text.				
Someone	Wants	But	So	Then

Figure 3: Plot Line

A second more detailed level is a line diagram of the plot line text structure.

Have students describe the exposition (story start with setting and characters), then the rising action (shown as a zigzag of events leading to the problem at its most intense), the climax, and then the falling action as the characters work toward resolution.

Literacy Connections for the Middle School and High School Newcomer: Non-fiction Text

Another important element of text structure is to understand how non-fiction texts are organized. Have students work in pairs to complete an organizer such as the one below in which they identify the key parts of a non-fiction text. This could involve a non-fiction picture or concept book about a content topic, such as the water cycle, solar system, historical event, etc.

Table 5: Non-Fiction Text Information

Title of the book	
Author	
Publisher and date of publication	
Page number of the table of contents	
List of chapters in the book	
Page numbers of the glossary	
Page numbers of the index	
One thing interesting in the book	

Fluency

Fluency is the ability to read with a relative ease and flow. When students struggle to pronounce words, or break phrases and sentences into unnatural chunks, it impacts their ability to comprehend. Native English speakers usually reach "fluency" about the end of grade 2 or into grade 3. With newcomers, there is no set time. Individuals who were literate in their home language will usually reach this stage much faster because they understand what skills are needed to understand a passage. Once they master the basic vocabulary and the syntax of English, they can read with a certain level of skill even if they don't understand each word. They will get the gist of the passage and can fill in the details as they read, with context or with a dictionary.

Literacy Connections for the Middle School and High School Newcomer

Provide middle and high school students with a text of two paragraphs, one familiar and one unfamiliar. Periodically have each newcomer read to the teacher, alternating between a familiar and unfamiliar text. Scribe anecdotal notes about the learner's pronunciation, pace, pauses, intonation, etc. Periodically review errors with each student and teach mini-lessons to all students related to the components of fluency.

Oral language

The main difference in learning to read in a second language as opposed to learning to read in a native language is the role of oral language. Native English speakers usually come to kindergarten or first grade with over 10,000 words in their oral vocabulary (Cárdenas-Hagan, 2020)! Newcomers may take years to reach this level. For newcomers who come after grade 3, mainstream classroom reading instruction does not usually include the typical basic phonic and phonemic skills because it is assumed that the students have already developed them. This means that the language teacher must infuse this aspect of reading into the already complex language development curriculum, and the higher the grade, the larger the gap between what oral vocabulary the student has and what they are expected to have and be able to use. Rather than focus on what cannot be changed, it is the role of the language development instructor to build oral language skills simultaneously with basic reading skills, academic vocabulary, and content knowledge.

Literacy Connections for the Middle School and High School Newcomer
Practicing oral language can be accomplished throughout each English lesson with activities such as turn and talk, sentence stems and sentence frames, think-pair-share and think-pair-share-square (see activity example in "Teaching Content to Newcomers," this chapter), as well as picture and text prompts to encourage oral responses to a question posed by the teacher or another newcomer.

Language Structures and Conventions

One aspect of oral language necessary to reading comprehension is syntax and grammar. Native speakers learn grammar intuitively through hearing their first language or L1 spoken and seldom know the rules behind their word choices. Understanding basic grammar is necessary for both reading and writing proficiency and should be a part of language development that must be taught simultaneously to word study.

Literacy Connections for the Middle School and High School Newcomer
Teaching grammar to newcomers should be linked to their reading and writing activities. It makes more sense to connect grammar structures to sentences in the texts students are learning. Mini grammar lessons help the learner make sense of the sentence components. It's important to carefully read through texts that students will be reading for the grammar structures important for both understanding the text and for extension activities, such as oral response and/or writing.

Vocabulary and Background Knowledge

Oral language knowledge correlates to vocabulary acquisition for all newcomers who are developing literacy while they are building speaking and listening skills. Most native speakers have a much greater oral language repertoire than their reading vocabulary, but for older newcomers, the opposite may be true. They may be able to read words that they have not yet heard in conversation.

Along with building a newcomer's vocabulary, teachers must also focus on extending a student's world schema through extensive and intensive reading. The more a student is exposed to new information, the greater their ability to tie new information to that which they already have. However, this new information must have some connection to previous experience for it to be understood and retained. It is a delicate balance to reach what Krashen (1982) called "comprehensible input," described as the formula $i + 1$. He argued that learning occurs when new information (the 1) is added or built upon current knowledge (the i). Current brain research confirms this theory, as it tells us that we must have something on which to tie or hang new information for it to be comprehensible and for us to remember it.

Literacy Connections for the Middle School and High School Newcomer

A strategy that can be applied to vocabulary and background knowledge, comprehension, cross-language connections, and writing is called "making text connections." There are three levels of text connections. They are text-to-text, text-to-self, and text-to-world.

For vocabulary, model for students how to make text connections related to words across the curriculum (text-to-text) and what experiences they have had with specific vocabulary (text-to-self and text-to-world); this would include words learned and what the words mean to them, as well as where they have heard them in their "world."

Comprehension

Most people argue that unless there is comprehension, there is no real reading, we only have word-calling. While being able to pronounce words is critical to reading, it is just the first step. It is the foundation of reading, but vocabulary, syntax, schema, etc. are the walls that make up the house. And just as learning a language is a time-intensive process for which there are no real shortcuts, so it is with developing reading comprehension. Becoming a skilled reader in a new language takes years, even if there are strong reading skills in the first language, and for those students without that foundation, it may take even longer. But a systemic, progressive program can help an individual to reach proficiency.

Literacy Connections for the Middle School and High School Newcomer

Similar to the strategies suggested for teaching vocabulary mentioned above, model for newcomers the connections between texts (text-to-text) they are reading with you. It could be connections between characters, settings, problems, resolutions, etc. Text-to-self connections could be about the characters, the setting, or the story problems and the students' own experiences. Text-to-world expands on text-to-self experiences, exploring what the newcomer knows about the world in their home country and/or their new country.

Cross-Language Connections

Even for students without home language literacy, there is a cross-language connection that must be taken into consideration when teaching reading. It effects the ability to hear the unfamiliar sounds of the new language and to make connections to the grammatical structures and vocabulary of English. It also informs the knowledge base that the reader brings to a text.

Writing

Writing must be developed along with reading as soon as possible for newcomers. Just as we cannot wait until the students obtain an oral vocabulary to begin to teach reading, so we cannot wait to teach writing. It is a critical skill that they will need each day in school, and learning it along with reading can help speed the process. Writing helps cement new ideas into the brain through the kinesthetic process of movement. Students who are preliterate may have to be taught to hold a pencil or pen, and individuals from languages that do not use the Roman alphabet will have to practice writing the new letters, but this can be a relatively quick process. Writing uses muscles just like any other activity, and it takes practice to develop small motor skills, but eventually this activity will pay dividends as the students build both aspects of literacy together.

Literacy Connections for the Middle School and High School Newcomer

To help newcomers craft their own original written texts, model from your own personal connections with the text and what you have learned in the world. Before actual writing takes place, students can talk through their ideas with a partner and/or the teacher one to one. For some of your newest students, you may need to scribe for them. Include word banks, sentence stems, and sentence frames to help them craft their own texts.

The Reading Rope

In 2001, Hollis Scarborough published a chapter in *The Handbook for Research in Early Literacy* in which the following now famous Reading Rope infographic appeared. She originally created this design out of pipe cleaners to help describe the various components of the reading process to parents of young children.

The top threads of the rope make up the five separate strands of knowledge about language required for reading, and the lower section of the rope is made up of the areas of word recognition that combine to create the various components of reading comprehension. Either section by itself is not sufficient, and when even one thread is missing, the rope loses its strength. For newcomers, it is even more critical that all threads are addressed simultaneously, since most students do not come with oral proficiency in English.

For this reason, it is vital that newcomers receive both English language development classes as well as a focus specifically on the basics of reading. Either one alone is not enough. Without time spent on both components of this rope, learning to read in English will be difficult. "It is a struggle to hear and isolate the sounds/phonemes of English, a challenge to understand the syntax and structure of English text, and difficult to comprehend and make meaning of vocabulary in a language they haven't learned. Designated English language development time should prepare for and respond to the linguistic demands English learners are facing in academic and literacy tasks throughout the curriculum" (Olsen, 2022, p. 4).

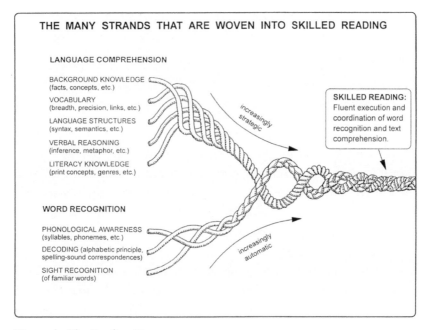

Figure 4: The Reading Rope

Scarborough, H. S. (2001). Connecting early language and literacy to later reading (dis)abilities: Evidence, theory, and practice. In S. Neuman & D. Dickinson (Eds.), *Handbook for research in early literacy* (pp. 97–110). New York: Guilford Press.
Used by permission from Guilford Press.

Literacy Instruction

Incorporating the basic components of literacy into daily lessons can be a challenge. In addition to knowing what to teach, the difficulty comes with how to teach these critical areas in a way that is comprehensible to newcomers without being presented through tedious drills, unconnected to vocabulary and/or content learning. There is also the issue that students are falling even farther behind their peers while concentrating on these foundational skills. The ideal solution is to somehow combine the content lessons into the literacy skill practice. Using picture books and easy concept books on topics that match the grade level curriculum is the best way to do this if you have enough students to create a small group or even a class. For example, a fourth grade class could focus on biographies of famous scientists. How to pronounce and spell the names of persons, places, key content words, and concepts could be part of the phonemic and phonics lesson for the day. They could learn about the invention of the telephone, the telegraph, the phonograph, and the television while learning about prefixes and root words. Timelines could help students practice pronouncing numbers. Students could be asked to orally summarize after completing a simple graphic organizer, followed by a co-writing, or dictating a short paragraph to a peer. This type of lesson builds the oral vocabulary of the student while giving them exposure and practice with all four language domains: listening, speaking, reading, and writing.

Numeracy Development for Newcomers

Numeracy is essentially the mathematical equivalent to literacy. Just as literacy is the basic knowledge of sounds and words that combine to express ideas, numeracy is the basic knowledge of numbers and symbols to express mathematical concepts. Numeracy is also teaching mathematical concepts while concurrently developing literacy skills, with a focus on math vocabulary development, oral and written comprehension, cultural competence, and comprehensible input.

Numeracy is more than just being able to manipulate numbers and mathematical symbols; it is also being able to maneuver the mathematics required for life in a modern society: telling time and following a calendar, making purchases, reading charts and graphs, understanding and using fractions, percent, estimation, and money. For school-age children, it is successfully navigating the coursework required for academic success leading to high school graduation and being prepared for post-secondary demands.

Numeracy is similar to literacy in that where you start, how much time you spend on each topic, and how much material you can cover depends on the student. Students with limited exposure to formal education will have only a rudimentary knowledge of mathematics. These students may need to start with primary level skills development, with a focus on math reasoning, and may require several years of math instruction to reach proficiency. Just as with literacy development, instruction should be based on the background knowledge of the student and build on previous competency.

Instruction for secondary students is doubly challenging because the math courses offered for students at this level assume a certain level of math proficiency. Some students arrive with only basic computational skills, while many high schools do not offer any math courses below algebra, such as general math or math assistance.

There are two ways that schools are addressing this issue. Some schools are adding an introductory level math course at grade 8 or 9, which prepares students for algebra. This course can be offered as an elective credit, when possible, since time is so critical for these students, and they need to obtain the required high school credits as soon as possible. Other schools, especially for students who have middle school level math skills, offer a double block of algebra. This has the advantage of giving students additional time and attention to building critical math skills while still providing required math credits. The first semester can be spent preparing students for the skills needed in algebra, and then the second semester can focus on the typical algebra curriculum in an extended time block for extra support.

The Myth of "Math Is Universal"

> Many people have the belief that the basics of mathematics are "universal" and therefore relatively easy for second language students to maneuver. This is often not the case.

The simple issue of how to write the numbers is not universal. What we call Arabic numerals are not those used in Arabic-speaking countries. They use numbers that look more like Babylonian cuneiform! And in most non-English speaking countries, the use of the comma and the decimal point in numbers are the opposite of that used in the United States and Canada. For example, two thousand four hundred dollars and fifteen cents would be written $2.400,15. Also, although long division results will always be the same, the process looks very different in many parts of the world.

Other typical differences include the measurement of time using local or religious calendars that do not mirror the Roman-based calendar of most Western nations. Many countries use what we call military time rather than the confusing a.m. and p.m. of the United States, based on a 24-hour day rather than two 12-hour half days. Dates in most areas of the world are written with the day first, then the month, and finally the year. (This can cause much confusion over birthdates!) And of course, the difference most noticeable to many Americans is the use of the metric system in almost every other part of the world. These examples help to show that learning math may be much more than just learning a new set of vocabulary labels for common concepts. Even mathematics has a cultural and societal base that cannot be ignored.

Word Problems

Word problems are traditionally the bane of the second language learner's math experience. "In mathematics, ESL students often make good progress in acquiring basic computation skills in the early grades. However, they typically experience greater difficulty in learning to interpret and solve work problems, and this difficulty increases in the later elementary grades as the word problems become more linguistically and conceptually complex" (Cummins, 2006). For newcomers, who must begin manipulating word problems while still at the beginning stages of English proficiency, the difficulty is even more profound.

Tips for Solving Word Problems

Teaching how to solve word problems for English learners should include the use of visuals, including pictures, graphics, and drawings, to help students "see" the problem. Pointing out multiple-meaning words such as "yard" and its meaning in the context of the problem can eliminate confusion: is it a unit of measurement or the land surrounding the house in which a garden is to be planted? Acting out the problem, through role play, with manipulatives, or in total physical response (TPR), can help students to discover the key elements required to solve it. Finally, it is important to teach students the art of eliminating unnecessary text in order to focus on the important vocabulary related to steps or processes (such as "average," "mean," "mode," "sum," etc.). Students often get caught up in figuring out what is a bowling alley, for example, in a problem involving finding the highest and lowest scores of the bowlers. It's important to help students understand that some words are not necessary to the solution.

Teaching Numeracy to Newcomers

Teaching numeracy to second language learners also requires certain skills. Many secondary math teachers are not trained for and often do not feel comfortable helping English language learners build the necessary foundational skills for numeracy success. Especially for students with limited formal schooling, the use of elementary methods and materials such as manipulatives and realia may be critical during the initial stages of instruction. In addition, consider using elementary literacy classroom aids, such as word walls, math journals, vocabulary games, and concept picture books, to build the linguistic base for math understanding.

Finally, numeracy can be combined with literacy development to tie these two seemingly disparate disciplines into one. Word walls have a place in a math classroom as much as in language arts. Vocabulary development is a critical component of both subjects. Visuals, gestures, and the use of the first language can complement and supplement oral and written instructions. Graphic organizers assist students to relate key concepts and sequence operational steps. Picture books containing shapes, designs, and math concepts can be used to introduce a lesson or assist a student who cannot yet visualize a lesson. Expecting students to write every day can build a student's math skills as much as it contributes to his/her language development. And having students create and solve their own word problems can help them realize how to deconstruct complex word problems created by others.

Literacy Connections for the Middle School and High School Newcomer: Some Life Skills Examples

Money
Practice with understanding the value of coins and bills; use advertisements and flyers to practice making purchases, determining total costs, using both bills and coins, and determining change, plus understanding place value and the vocabulary for expressing/understanding place value (tens, hundreds, thousands, etc.). Practice estimating the total cost of purchases, such as clothing or a meal in a restaurant, before calculating the actual cost.

Time
Practice with understanding time in terms of 12 or 24 hours. Then, practice with schedules (train, bus, school) and understanding elapsed time. How much time will pass from the start to the end? How long will a train take to get to another city? Introduce percent, fractions, and decimals here in terms

of dividing up the day into how many activities and how much time each involves: "I am in school six hours, which is 25% or ¼ of my day."

Measurement

Practice measuring with a tape measure, ruler, yardstick, as well as liquid measurements; include modeling estimation in comparison to actual measurement. Explore shapes and introduce vocabulary when using measurement for squares, triangles, rectangles, cubes, hexagons, etc. from the classroom environment. Create measurement word problems in a real-world environment, which can include geometric shapes and sizes. Measure the amount of area needed in a yard to create a doghouse or a garden.

With all these examples, actual tools/realia (e.g., money, clocks, train/bus schedules, rulers, yardsticks, tape measures, liquid measuring cups, and spoons) help the middle school and secondary newcomer understand the concepts for each of these mathematical topics before moving on to algebra and geometry.

Teaching Content to Newcomers

Strategies such as those used in sheltered instruction and in structured lesson planning and assessment programs such as Sheltered Instruction Observation Protocol (SIOP, a lesson-delivery model) can help students learn mathematics content. Sheltered instruction focuses on building background knowledge, interactions between peers and teachers, as well as practice activities. Vocabulary word maps, such as the Frayer model, help students understand definitions, often written collaboratively by students; visual examples and non-examples; as well as student-generated sentences using the key words. Interactive activities such as think-pair-share and think-pair-share-square provide opportunities to work with peers to practice and solve mathematics problems. Think-pair-share-square expands interaction activities beyond the small group into another share level to practice both math vocabulary and problem solving.

Think-Pair-Share-Square Example

ELs have a word problem involving elapsed time. The problem includes a starting time and an ending time. They read the problem and share their understanding of the problem with a partner (pair share). As a pair, they solve the problem with a manipulative, such as a clock, noting the starting time and ending time and counting the hours and minutes between start and end. Before sharing with the entire ESL class, the pair share their process and results with another pair (square share). Coming to consensus on the correct answer, the four students (both pairs) describe and explain their results to the EL classroom. The teacher may provide all students with sentence starters to support their oral explanations when sharing.

Word walls with key math language can help students to form questions, explain their answers, and answer questions from peers and the teacher. Project- and problem-based learning activities in math built around long-term learning, including connections to reading, and centered around student interests help to improve math understanding and build learning across the curriculum.

Self-Study or Group Study Activities

1. Literacy development activities for multilingual newcomers in middle school and high school need to connect individual skills learning with academic vocabulary and content learning. Consider the components below and reflect on how you could approach each to teach both literacy skills and incorporate academic vocabulary and content learning for newcomers.

   Table 6: Components of a Literacy Program

Literacy component	Middle School	High School
Phonics/decoding/word work		
Knowledge of text structures		
Fluency and/or oral language		
Language structures		
Concepts of print		

2. Earlier in the chapter we describe how to use think-pair-share and think-pair-share-square with content learning. Think-pair-share-square can be used with mathematics problem solving. Think of how you could model the strategy for a group of multilingual newcomers solving a word problem. First, find or create a typical word problem in a text. Then, think about how you could demonstrate the steps in the problem orally, visually, and with manipulatives. What happens the first time you teach it, and then what would this problem look like using think-pair-share and think-pair-share-square?

CHAPTER THREE

Instructional Strategies and Classroom Activities for Newcomers

Best Practice Number Three: Develop the classroom supports necessary for students to achieve academic success.

Welcoming New Students

When students first arrive, make every effort to help them feel comfortable and welcome. Take them on a tour of the school (find a student who speaks the same language, if possible, to lead the tour so they can see the school through the eyes of a student). Focus on the layout of the school: the bathrooms, office, nurse, attendance area, gym, and cafeteria. For students who have not previously used technology, you will need to demonstrate how laptops operate and when they are to be used. Students may not be familiar with reading a schedule and may need a buddy for the first few days or weeks to help navigate the building. And at the end of the day, make sure a teacher, administrator, or member of the support staff is helping the student find the bus, and let the driver know the student is new and speaks little or no English. You may want to provide the student with a card with their name, address, phone number, and bus stop to use for the first few days or even weeks.

Where to Begin Instruction

All newcomers with beginning levels of English proficiency will need basic survival English—both speaking and reading. Start with the alphabet, sight words, basic oral vocabulary words such as greetings, basic survival questions, their address and phone number, colors, numbers, food, body parts, family members, school vocabulary, etc. Practicing basic survival questions such as: Where is the bathroom? The nurse's office? The lunchroom? The bus? is critical. Students will need repetition and drills until they get used to hearing and responding to English, at least for a few weeks. Visuals, gestures, videos (such as those on YouTube), movement, and games can be invaluable. Reading aloud to students and using books with numerous pictures, even at the secondary level, gives students the opportunity to hear fluent English and become familiar with the sounds of English. Graphs, charts, flash cards, and photos provide additional support for students at all grade levels and in every subject.

Checklist for Welcoming Students

The following list of suggested practices for welcoming students into your school is adapted from the video *Tips for Welcoming Newcomers*, made by Amber Prentice, (ColorinColorado, 2012). If your school does not yet do some of these practices, who could you contact to discuss adding them to your welcome package?

Table 7: Checklist for Welcoming Newcomers

	Is the school entrance clearly marked and welcoming?
	Does someone provide EL families and students with school tour and orientation in home language?
	Are security measures understandable to EL families (e.g., illustrations and/or in multiple languages)?
	Does your school have bilingual staff or a phone or video interpretation service available to assist families?
	Is the interpretation service or language assistance evident in the office?
	Does your school have signs in other languages?
	Is there evidence of welcoming other countries/cultures (e.g., flags, maps, cultural artifacts, art displays)?
	Do staff members treat all families courteously?
	Are all relevant staff members informed about new students' languages, cultures, and initial screening data?
	Do the school library and classrooms have books in other languages?
	Does your school or district have an EL family webpage with resources?
	Does your school have multicultural events? How do you inform the families of these events?

The Hidden Curriculum

> The *hidden curriculum* is defined as the unspoken, implicit values, accepted behaviors, and norms that exist within an educational setting. (Jackson, 1968)

The hidden curriculum is generally not part of the academic curriculum in the school setting, making it difficult to understand or internalize since it is not written, modeled, clearly explained, or easily understood by learners. This is especially true for newcomers and SLIFE. It affects how English learners adjust to their new school environment, understand learning time (e.g., whole class, small group, pair, and independent learning classroom configurations), ask for help, perceive how school "works," interact with teachers and other learners, and know to complete assignments.

Here are a few hidden curriculum elements that if explained would help English learners make a smoother transition into US schools.

- **Interpreting and understanding teacher directions**: It is important to provide clear and complete directions for every assignment. English learners, especially in middle and high school, need to know how to complete an assignment. These everyday classroom work procedures are rarely understood by the newcomer without initial and repeated explanations as well as clear modeling of expectations, with visual examples when possible. In addition, tone of voice, facial expressions, and body language can be bewildering to the newcomer and convey a message that confuses and blocks potential future communication between the teacher and newcomer because English learners may have difficulty reading these "unspoken messages." Avoid cursive if possible.

- **Questioning**: Newcomers do not ask questions partly because they are just learning how to speak English, make requests, and formulate questions in English. In addition, many come from native countries in which questioning a teacher is not acceptable. They must be specifically taught how and when to ask questions. Question stems can be included in a student's notebook to help students understand and remember for future use.

- **Working in groups**: In US schools there are many times when students are asked to work with a partner or in a group of three to four others. Teachers need to ensure that all students have clear instructions about the expectation and the process of how to engage in working with others on assignments, group projects, and paired reading, research and/or question response activities. It is important to model and reinforce the rules of how to take turns, how to divide up the assignment, what product is expected from the group, and how to form and communicate opinion statements. Especially during the first several months, teachers will need to determine which assignment parts and products the newcomer can and will be able to complete with sample models, word banks, sentence frames/stems, and/or a combination of drawing and language.

Understanding school norms: The hidden curriculum assumes that newcomers understand their role as students and know how to move within the school, within a classroom, from class to class, to the lunchroom, at recess or in physical education classes. In many other cultures and countries, it is the teachers who move and students do not move within the school building from class to class, or even within a classroom. Often other cultures expect students to sit in one place throughout the lesson. They are expected to listen to the teacher, and only the teacher, for the information being explained. Therefore, some English learners will be confused and resistant to working cooperatively and collaboratively with peers, because a peer is not the teacher.

Additionally, although there may be dress codes within a school, choices of clothing, footwear, and bookbags may not be expressly communicated. Many English learners attended schools in which they wore uniforms and textbooks were not taken home. These aspects of school life that US educators consider conventional are all part of unfamiliar or unknown norms for new English learners. Providing an orientation to the expectations in each school in terms of appropriate school dress; care of school property, such as textbooks, workbooks, school equipment (technology and school tools, such as lab equipment); lunchroom procedures; hallway movement; visits to the school nurse; restroom passes; as well as how to behave during various school drills is important.

Even the norms of how to properly use the restroom may cause confusion. How to contact the school due to illness, as well as transportation-related questions (e.g., busing locations, expected bus behavior) and other situations, requires clear directions for both students and their families in their native language and/or with the assistance of a translator.

Interacting with bullies: Bullying is a serious problem for EL newcomers. Knowing very little of the language in their new school, they could be taken advantage of by another student posing as a potential friend. This is a serious concern and should be something that teachers, aides, and support staff monitor in the school. Checking in with newcomers and assisting them with developing strategies to make new friends and prevent them from becoming the object of bullying is key to helping them overcome social obstacles.

Providing opportunities for newcomers and native English speakers to develop friendships will enhance the overall school culture. The well-being and social development of all students is truly the goal. One way to do this is through paired or cooperative learning activities, school clubs, and extra-curricular activities, including sports, all of which create a welcoming environment. The US government has an official website with some valuable information on bullying that may be helpful: www.stopbullying.gov.

Building orientation: For English learners, their first impressions upon entering a school either make them feel welcome, prepare them to overcome obstacles to learning, or cause them to worry about fitting in. What helps? Native language student ambassadors, when possible, who lead a tour of the school for the student and the family, which would include restrooms, nurse's office, and physical education, art, music, and technology facilities. A team of student ambassadors available as needed will help the newcomer adjust to the hidden curriculum from the student viewpoint. Student ambassadors can create a school club and be acknowledged with service learning credit for their volunteer work. Training of student ambassadors is key to the program's success.

Exposing the hidden curriculum to new arrivals and ensuring that there is a school-wide transformation for multilingual learners and the community is the responsibility of the entire school. It requires embracing change and seeing this change as an opportunity to make the school a safer place for all students. This mindset creates a vision for equal access for English learners' families, newcomers, and SLIFE, as well as for all learners in the school community.

Vignette: Ayana, 14, from Japan, arrives with her parents to register and begin attending her first American middle school. They enter the building and find that the school has posted signs in many different languages, including Japanese, as well as flags, artwork, and pictures from many countries of students in the school. The family is happily surprised. When they enter the front office, the secretary greets them in English but also provides some orientation material, including a school handbook of rules and a campus map, as well as directions for registration, in English and Japanese. The ESL teacher and a student ambassador (a former ESL student who speaks Japanese) arrive to greet the family. The ESL teacher introduces herself and provides the family with a brochure describing the school's ESL program in English and Japanese. The student ambassador takes the family on a tour of the school, explaining key information needed for Ayana's first few weeks of school. She concludes the tour at the front office and explains to the family that she plans to meet Ayana the following morning to take her to the ESL classroom, where she will be paired with another student who will have the same classes and travel with her for the first few weeks.

Supporting Students' Cultures: How to Be a Culturally Proficient Teacher of Newcomers

There is more to supporting the cultures of the students than simply hanging flags in the hallway. It must go deeper and be imbedded in the planning and delivery of daily lessons. Zaretta Hammond, in her recent book *Culturally Responsive Teaching and the Brain* (2014), describes why creating a welcoming atmosphere is critical to learning. She encourages teachers to consider these statements when designing their classrooms:

- Positive relationships keep us feeling safe and allow us to be open to learning.

- Attention drives learning. We must have an atmosphere of acceptance and of "comprehensible input" for students to be able to concentrate.

- All new information must be coupled to existing "funds of knowledge" to be learned; therefore, we need to begin by finding out what students already know on a subject and what they need to learn next (i + 1).

In her book, Hammond explains that our bodies are hard-wired for protection and that we have reflexes that kick in when we feel threatened with the unknown. For newcomers, that could describe much of their school day. The more that teachers and staff can help students feel safe and welcome, the more they are physically able to concentrate on academic tasks.

Instructional Strategies and Classroom Activities for Newcomers 59

We also must tie new information to what the student already has implanted in their brain, their previous school knowledge, so we need to start each new topic with connections to prior learning (whether school facts or life experiences). The Progression of Instruction listed below provides a framework for moving newcomers from orientation to integration with mainstream curriculum.

Progression of Instruction Based on Language Proficiency

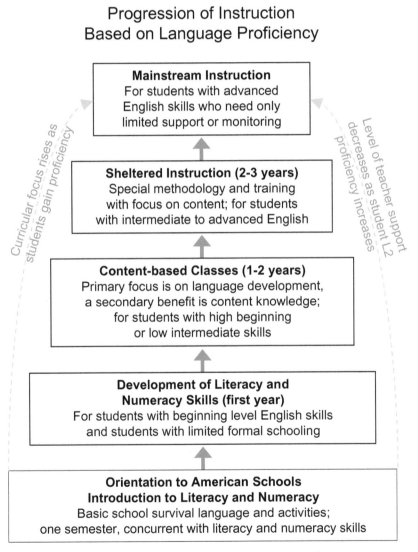

Figure 5: Progression of Instruction Based on Language Proficiency
(Begin with orientation to American schools and work up from the bottom of the pyramid.)

Instructional Strategies and Supports for New Arrivals

As the English language proficiency of the student grows, the types of strategies and supports will require changes. Basic literacy and numeracy will morph into lessons that are closer to grade level curriculum, based on state standards. The graphic above shows the stages that students will move through as their English and their content knowledge develops. These stages are fluid and often overlap. For example, the initial orientation to school is happening at the same time as basic literacy and numeracy skills are being introduced (if students are SIFE/SLIFE). For students with a strong educational background who just need to build their English skills, this first step may only take a few weeks, and they may be able to skip the second step altogether. These students may be able to jump almost immediately into sheltered instruction, only needing language support as they move into grade level courses. And for programs with bilingual courses and strategy instruction, they may move directly into grade appropriate courses taught in the home language until their English has progressed sufficiently for mainstream instruction. Each student's situation must be given individual consideration.

Build upon Prior Knowledge

Whatever the skills and academic experiences that students come with, you need to start each new topic or unit by discovering what students already know about a topic and what skills they already possess. This is often referred to as activating or accessing prior knowledge or background knowledge. There are several ways to find out what students already know so that you can start the lesson at the proper level or so you can tie the new information to what students already have learned. First, you can simply ask! You can ask questions that elicit from students what they already know about a subject and how much (see chart below). For example, you could put a term such as "monarchy" on the board and ask students what the word means and what they already know about monarchs. You could show a picture of a king or queen that they might recognize and ask follow-up questions. You could show a short video of King Charles at his coronation and ask if they know who this is and what is happening. This part of the lesson should take only a couple minutes, but using photos, videos, and other visual supports can allow students with more limited English to participate in the lesson and understand what the lesson will be about. Then record their responses on a chart labeled "K" for what they already know and "W" for what they want to learn about the topic.

Additionally, you could use an online dictionary, such as www.merriam-webster.com, to explore definitions and examples and to hear words pronounced. Then, as students learn about monarchies, you can add a third column and expand to a KWL chart, which then includes "L" for what they have learned. An advanced version would include a fourth column for "W": where they learned the information. In this way, you are differentiating for the ability level of the newcomer.

Table 8: KWL Chart

What I know	What I want to learn	What I learned and where I learned it

Teach Language and Content Simultaneously

Two of the steps on the language progression ladder above involve teaching content while building English language skills (Content-Based Classes and Sheltered Instruction). Again, these two language methods can be utilized simultaneously and should be whenever possible. This is especially critical for secondary educators who are working against the clock to close the gap between what the students already know and what they are expected to be able to do. In a content-based class, the focus is on language development through content. For example, a middle school ESL class may read the chapter book *The Circuit* by Francisco Jiménez. The book is an autobiography about the author's life as a migrant worker's son during the mid-1900s. Along with the book discussion, the class could work on maps, timelines, and the push-pull factors of immigration (skills and topics needed in a social studies class). They can also listen to an online reading of chapters from *The Circuit* and/or Francisco Jiménez talking about the book on YouTube.

In a sheltered class, the focus is on the subject, and the grade is based on the content area. In the example given above, a middle school social studies class could read a chapter from *The Circuit* with the idea that the class will look at the role of migrant farmers and their economic benefit in American society. The lesson may be similar, but the focus is different. In both cases, the newcomer will be building critical skills in both language and content.

In both types of classes, similar supports will be essential for newcomers and other language learners. Visuals are critical for all English learners, but they are especially critical for new arrivals. Visuals include gestures, photos, clip art, short film clips, graphs, and charts. With modern technology, adding visuals to a lesson is easier than ever. Visuals can also include realia, such as real or plastic fruits and vegetables, play or real money, stuffed animals, puppets, menus, clothing, etc. The types of realia will vary depending on the age of the student and the content subject.

Employ Graphic Organizers

One type of support that benefits newcomers and more proficient language learners alike is a graphic organizer. There are hundreds of variations of graphic organizers, with the most common being a web, a T-chart, a sequence chart, a Venn diagram, a Frayer vocabulary model, a concept map, a plot line, timeline, and multiple column charts. There are several benefits of using graphic organizers with newcomers: these graphic organizers only require simple English, they help students easily make connections and see relationships, they can help students sort items into categories, they can serve as an outline for simple paragraphs, and they are less threatening than asking students to write extensive notes. As with other supports, it is important that the first time a new type of organizer is used, the teacher model its use and explain how to transfer the information from the lesson to the condensed version to be placed on the organizer. Being able to determine what information is important takes practice and a certain level of language proficiency. For the newest students, the teacher may need to select the information, place it on the graphic organizer in the correct location, and explain each step orally. This can also be done in pairs or small groups, if the students truly work together and don't simply have the more proficient do the work for the newer arrivals.

Utilize Peer Assistance and Group Work

Having students work in pairs or small groups is an excellent way to gradually move new students into the rhythm and fabric of the class. It is important that the groups be teacher selected, at least part of the time, with the intention of having students with stronger English language skills assist their peers with less proficiency. However, choosing students with the personality and interest to help others is more important than strictly looking at English proficiency or matching peers by home language. It is also necessary to allow the students to choose their own groups sometimes, giving them some control over their learning environment.

Focus on Vocabulary

Another important strategy to help new arrivals better understand a lesson is to introduce key vocabulary in advance of the lesson. The vocabulary, including words, pictures, examples, and non-examples, provides the foundation for learning content. Presenting a list of five to seven words that are important to the lesson can help all the students in the class, not just the newcomers. Focus especially on words that can be "teachable moments," like multiple-meaning words, words with prefixes or roots, words that are cognates, polysemous words, and words connected to a content topic introduced in ESL or mainstream or content classes.

Multiple-meaning words or **polysemous** words are words that mean different things in different circumstances and can cause difficulty for English learners. Look at the list below and think about how these common words can mean something different in a math, science, or history class. A student who knows the common meaning may be confused when confronted with the same word in a textbook.

Table 9: Multiple-Meaning or Polysemous Words Chart

Multiple-meaning word	Common usage	Specific content usage	Specific content usage
Ruler	a stick for measuring	leader of a country	
Bank	a place to keep money	side of a river	save for later
Log	a piece of wood	sign-in on a computer	a journal entry
Cell	a small phone	smallest part of a plant or animal	a room in the jail
Date	a day on a calendar	going with a person to an event	fruit

List three additional polysemous words that are commonly used in your content area or grade level and the various meanings for each, including slang. How might you teach these?

Math Vocabulary

Math especially has many ways to say the same thing, causing difficulties, especially with word problems. Think about how many words mean to add:

- addition
- altogether
- combine
- total
- increase
- sum
- all
- in all
- more than
- plus
- both

Creating anchor charts with a list of the many terms to express addition, subtraction, multiplication, and division can help students tackle at least one confusing part of understanding a word problem. Many of these lists can be found on the internet for free.

Mathematics Application Activity

The words "yard," "foot," and "plot" have multiple meanings in mathematics and other content areas. Have your students create a word problem with one of these words and any additional words that may have multiple meanings. Which cognates would help the most for students to understand the problem? How might you explain the meanings in words and visuals and even TPR for and with your students?

Cognates

Another area of vocabulary development for newcomers is the recognition and use of **cognates**. Many words in English come from Latin or Greek, often through French or Spanish. So many of these words look or even sound like the words in the home language that it is critical that the connection be made when using the words in class. Often students will not make this connection if it is not deliberately pointed out to them. These words are especially prevalent between Spanish and English in math, science, and social studies.

Table 10: Common Spanish Cognates Chart

General school words	Math cognates	Science cognates	History cognates
activity/actividad	minute/minuto	plant/planta	nation/nación
definition/definición	day/día	action/acción	map/mapa
lesson/lección	double/doble	adapt/adaptar	north/norte
page/pagina	quarter/cuarto	asteroid/asteroide	continent/continente
practice/practicar	minus/menos	atomic/atómica	island/isla
section/seccion	calculate/calcular	biology/biología	ocean/océano
vocabulary/vocabulario	equal/igual	laboratory/laboratorio	hemisphere/hemisferio
class/clase	equation/ecuación	microscope/microscopio	geography/geografía
describe/describir	fraction/fracción	nucleus/núcleo	valley/valle

Word Banks

For students at the beginning or emerging level, providing a **word bank** allows students to access new vocabulary for classwork or tests. A word bank is a list of words needed for an assignment or test accommodation that can be referred to as key vocabulary and concept words for a unit of instruction. They can be placed at the top or bottom of the page in an assignment, be included as part of a word wall, be seen virtually on a class page, or listed on a whiteboard or bulletin board. This type of visual scaffold allows students to focus on the assignment rather than stressing over trying to remember so many new words.

Other suggested classroom support strategies:

- Extended time for classroom activities and assessments
- Simplifying the language of the assignment or decreasing the amount of work required
- Breaking down tasks to be completed in multiple sessions, rather than one class session
- Manipulatives
- Games
- Adapted texts
- Translated versions of texts
- Translation software/apps

Use Accommodations and Modifications

Accommodations are supports that a teacher provides that enable students to better understand a concept or provide evidence that they have mastered a topic; in other words, they promote comprehensible input to the student and comprehensible output from the student. Accommodations work best when students have some familiarity with a topic or skill and have a working knowledge of what is expected of them. Modifications are for students who need more extensive support, for example, a SLIFE with limited educational experience who has been placed in an algebra class. Until the student has a basic level of mathematics knowledge and skill, accommodations will probably not be sufficient. The student may need individual tutoring, a class on basic math, or a SLIFE pre-algebra class to build their background knowledge before being placed in algebra. Providing modifications may require individualized scheduling, problems and problems solving introduced in multiple lessons, and/or flexible grading for a period. Accommodations are more adaptable and are usually left to the discretion of the teacher.

Table 11: Typical Accommodations and Modifications

Accommodations—Examples for Newcomers	Modifications—Examples for Newcomers
Providing peer support (in native language when available and appropriate)	Changing expectations based on language proficiency level at the time of instruction
Employing visuals, graphics, manipulatives, realia, models	Reducing complexity and/or the expectation for performance on a lesson or assignment, including more time on task
Using gestures	Dividing an assignment into parts and/or stages and grading each separately
Supplying a native language dictionary, native language texts, or translated text information	Having the student complete similar types of assignments at a lower grade level at first
Using word banks, word walls, sentence stems, or sentence frames (cloze), word banks	Using prompts, cues, word banks, reduced amount and length of text for expected response
Giving extended wait time	Reading to the student individually and using targeted questioning to elicit responses; grading based on oral response
Using advanced organizers and guided notes	Using a targeted assignment rubric

Apply the Gradual Release of Responsibility Model

Most teachers are familiar with the concept of the gradual release of responsibility, in which learners who are new to a subject or topic begin by listening to a whole-group lesson presented by the teacher. After the initial introduction and explanation, the class practices using the new information together with the teacher's support. Eventually, the students perform or understand the new information well enough to be able to work independently. Some teachers call this "I Do, We Do, You Do." Many variations of this teaching model are available online.

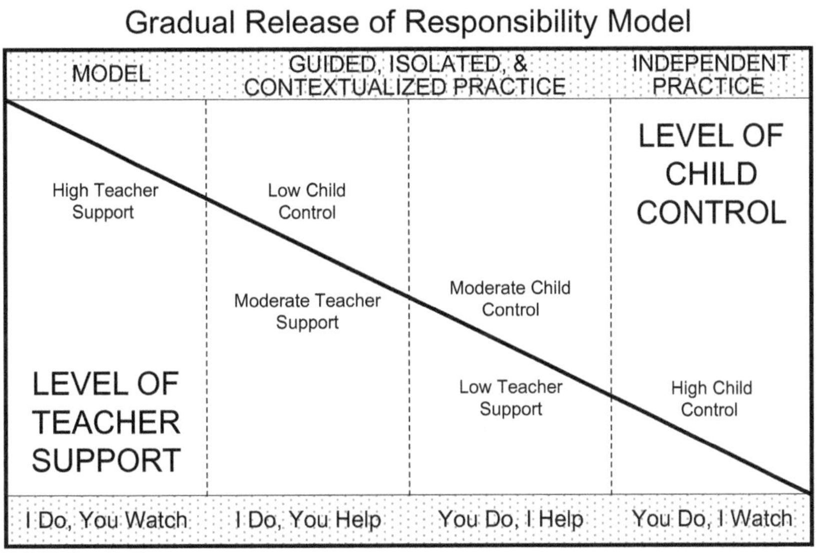

Gradual Release of Responsibility Model

MODEL	GUIDED, ISOLATED, & CONTEXTUALIZED PRACTICE		INDEPENDENT PRACTICE
High Teacher Support	Low Child Control		**LEVEL OF CHILD CONTROL**
	Moderate Teacher Support	Moderate Child Control	
LEVEL OF TEACHER SUPPORT		Low Teacher Support	High Child Control
I Do, You Watch	I Do, You Help	You Do, I Help	You Do, I Watch

Figure 6: Gradual Release of Responsibility Model (introduced by Pearson and Gallagher in 1983 and used with permission)

Promote Translanguaging

Freeman, Freeman, Soto, and Ebe (2016) tell us that translanguaging is the typical way bilinguals use language as they communicate in their communities. Multilingual learners think simultaneously in both their native or first language and English and use their first or native language to help them learn English. For example, "a student could be reading an article about the solar system in English, but in their brain, they are also thinking and making connections in Spanish" or another native language (Najarro, 2023).

> Translanguaging is the fluid movement between languages that allows newcomers to utilize their first language expertise to support their learning of the new language and content.

Seltzer, Garcia, and Ibarra Johnson (2016) refer to this as a "linguistic repertoire" that multilinguals have; creating "one complex linguistic system" that "has features of two or more languages" (p. 21).

Concurrent translation and the strategic use of translanguaging are not the same. In concurrent translation, an ESL or bilingual teacher translates instruction while teaching in English. It has been found to be an ineffective approach to teaching English or any second or additional language. Multilingual students who are taught through concurrent translation often "wait" for the teacher to explain directions, concepts and/or content vocabulary, and academic information to be explained in the native language. In contrast, translanguaging is strategic. The use of the native language is incorporated into understanding the concepts and gist of text. Students use native language to make sense of, for example, grammatical structures in English. Both languages are used simultaneously to construct meaning in English.

Vignette: Two multilingual students who speak the same first language collaboratively work on an assigned word problem. They become stuck on one of the words in English. They then think of the equivalent word in their native language to help them make sense of the word problem and what it is asking them to do. When tapping into one's native language with translanguaging support, students are not looking for word-to-word meaning but rather using the native language knowledge to help make sense of English instruction. As Stelzer et al. state: "translanguaging is a bilingual speaker's creative and critical construction and use of interrelated language features" (pp. 20-21). Bilingual learners use translanguaging to learn both content and language in the school setting to make sense of their learning.

Teach to Standards

The higher the grade level and the lower the previous education of the newcomer, the greater the challenge when trying to teach to grade level state standards. Obviously, mastery of these standards should be the goal for every teacher; we want all our students working at grade level and making steady progress. However, for some students this may be more of a challenge than for others. Students with interrupted schooling and students who are at the beginning or emerging level of English proficiency will need additional time and experience to be expected to perform at a level equal to their peers with consistent schooling in English. But that does not mean we ignore the standards and focus only on foundational skills. Standards need to be the goal in every subject and at every grade. Instruction for newcomers and for SLIFE can be seen as rungs on a ladder. Each step up the ladder leads to the goal of mastery of the grade level standard. Daily lessons can include the vocabulary and the skills needed for that mastery, and by spiraling the lessons, students can make steady progress up the ladder. Spiraling lessons means that a topic is covered in increasing detail as the lesson is repeated. For example, in a physical science class, the students could begin the year with learning the water cycle, and later in the year students could revisit the topic and focus on evaporation and condensation or water conservation. Finally, the students could end the year by reading about and discussing how agriculture is impacted by the water cycle or periods of drought. With each lesson, the vocabulary is revisited, and the reading level and the writing expectations of the students increases in difficulty.

Co-Teaching for Newcomers

Co-teaching is being implemented more frequently in elementary grade-level and/or middle school and secondary content classrooms to address diverse learning needs for all students, including multilingual newcomers and SLIFE learners. This method of instruction is most effective with students who have different instructional needs. Teachers in co-teaching settings bring together the expertise of the content teacher and the English language specialist. The National Education Association recently offered "Five Tips for Co-Teaching" (Gross, 2022) to make co-teaching partnerships work best. They are:

- **Establish Trust**—Co-teachers need to be able to trust one another by getting to know each other's strengths so that they can make the most of the partnership, knowing that they are both there to support the learners.
- **Start Strong with How You Present Yourselves to the Students**—Both teachers must present a united front of beliefs, classroom policies, and grading, as well as classroom discussions and conversations. All classroom materials should display both teachers' names.

- **Plan Together**—Although the classroom or content teacher is the content expert, the English language teacher has knowledge about the multilingual newcomers and SLIFE learners and which strategies, accommodations, and modifications work best. Common planning time is essential to ensure the success of all learners. Honigsfeld and Dove (2017) indicate the four key components of co-teaching to be: co-planning, co-instructing, co-assessing, and co-reflecting).

- **Think About Which Co-Teaching Model to Use**—There are a variety of models that can be used in co-taught lessons. Both teachers may take on different roles in a co-taught lesson. Teachers should not feel that only one model should be used in every lesson. See below for a description of various co-teaching models.

- **Be Flexible**—Know that all lessons may not work perfectly. Pay attention to students' needs and adjust lesson implementation as needed. Co-teaching, if done well, enables students to receive the attention they need to learn.

English Learner Co-Teaching Configurations

Andrea Honigsfeld and Maria Dove, specialists in co-teaching for English learner populations, describe the following possible co-teaching configurations in their 2017 book, *Co-Teaching for English Learners*. Keep in mind that in each scenario, the general education teacher may not always take the lead role. When working with newcomers, the lead teacher may be an ESL teacher with a more proficient group, joined by a teacher or para who focuses on the new arrivals, or the sheltered content teacher of ELs may be working with a teacher who has a newcomer or SLIFE group. The authors provide examples for teaching one group, two groups, or multiple groups.

- **One group: One lead teacher and one teacher "teaching on purpose"**—"Teaching on purpose" means that one of the teachers provides short, content-focused mini-lessons for a single student or a small group while the other teacher works with the rest of the class.

- **One group: Two teachers teach the same content**—Both teachers work together to teach the lesson, at the same time, adding clarification on concepts, vocabulary, examples, or extensions on key ideas within the lesson.

- **One group: One teaches, one assesses**—The teacher who is assessing focuses on observing the students, individually or as a group, through checklists, anecdotal notes, and/or running records.

- **Two groups: Two teachers teach same content**—Each teacher works with a heterogeneous group to provide time for interaction, coming to consensus on content answers and the monitoring of student learning.

- **Two groups: One teacher pre-teaches, one teacher teaches alternative information**—The teacher doing the pre-teaching focuses on the ESL students with missing background knowledge, while the other teacher can do enrichment. The ESL students could focus on essential vocabulary while the other group is expanding their vocabulary.

- **Two groups: One teacher re-teaches, one teacher teaches alternative information**—Only students needing additional learning time for reinforcement will be in the re-teaching group, while the alternative group will receive enrichment. Each group is heterogenous (English learners and other learners).

- **Multiple groups: Two teachers monitor and teach**—All students are grouped heterogeneously according to specific skill-based instructional needs. Teachers rotate from group to group providing mini-lessons and increased opportunities for student participation, engagement, and meaningful interaction. Students can rotate with their group since this model is often used for learning centers or learning stations.

In their work, specifically designed to respond to English learner needs through co-teaching, Honigsfeld and Dove provide co-teachers with a set of core beliefs. They state that both teachers must:

- have a shared philosophy of teaching
- use consistent and supportive teaching practices
- bridge and build content knowledge
- believe in collaborative practice
- possess cross-cultural and interpersonal skills
- support the learner using linguistic adaptations

Assessment: Showcasing Student Growth through Multiple Measures of Data

It is important to know how much growth newcomers and SLIFE are making and in what areas. The best way to understand this is to go beyond a single annual assessment and explore multiple measures of data:

1. Are English learners progressing toward English proficiency?
2. Are the gaps between new arrivals and current English learners getting smaller? It is important to view the size of the gap, rates of achievement over time, and progress toward closing the gap.
3. Are English learners making progress toward meeting standards?
4. What have you implemented that has positively influenced and produced better outcomes?

All these questions are key to understanding if your program is working and if your formal and informal assessments help you, the teacher, to fine tune your instruction to reach all the newcomers and/or SLIFE in your program.

Authentic assessments are assessments based on actual learning in the classroom, whether language learning or content learning or both. Building assessments into instruction, with a variety of authentic assessment tasks, provides the teacher with an understanding of what has been understood and learned.

Yzquierdo (2017) divides authentic assessments for newcomers into two categories: What the teacher creates or uses and what the newcomer creates or uses. The teacher's authentic assessments should include rubrics, checklists, and observational tools, such as notes from teacher-student and student-student interactions, progress portfolios, and any other ways to note progress toward the achievement of content.

What the newcomer creates could include drawings, audio or video recordings, academic projects, and learning logs. To determine newcomer understanding of content and to note language development, students can complete graphic organizers, KWL charts, reflection journals, timelines, and self-evaluations. In addition, teachers can include English language or native language word banks (e.g., cognates), word-to-word dictionaries, and one-to-one responses shared with a partner or teacher who scribes the responses on the tool being used.

Traditional assessments are designed to assess content understanding and are usually based on a content learning unit. Much of what is taught to newcomers is taught with accommodations for their current level of oral and written language, based on their ability to understand aurally presented information. The traditional pen/pencil and paper assessments should also provide accommodations for the newcomer. Some examples of accommodations include:

- Glossaries, bilingual word-for-word dictionaries (requires teaching and modeling to show students how to use these tools during instruction)
- Visuals, pictures, and/or diagrams labeled (partially or completely, to accompany assessment questions)
- Study guides (in simplified English with extensively labeled illustrations, etc.) to help the newcomer understand the content better—used both with instruction and to prepare for pencil and paper assessments—can be used during pencil and paper assessments, as well. This is similar to an open-book test for more advanced learners.
- Allowing more time on an assessment or breaking assessments into smaller chunks of time or into smaller, topic-specific sections.
- Assessment in a one-on-one setting: teacher and student, English-speaker student scribe and newcomer, or proficient native first language speaker as scribe and newcomer
- Allowing students to produce sequenced pictures in response to questions with steps or stages related to content, such as science experiments or a timeline in social studies
- Allowing students to place information cards in correct sequential order to answer a test question or match vocabulary word cards with definitions and/or illustrations matching meaning

Self-Study or Group Study Activities

1. **School manual:** Consider creating a simplified school manual or handbook for newcomers that could be used with English learners and other newcomers to your school. Design a table of contents that would be most helpful to dispel the issues of a hidden curriculum. Work with colleagues, if possible. Complete wording for one chapter. What illustrations and/or photographs would be helpful?

Who in your community could accurately translate the manual into first languages of newcomers?

2. **Assessment:** Think about a lesson you have recently taught and how you assessed your learners. Consider the assessment suggestions mentioned in the chapter. Think of one or two students who would benefit from a different type of assessment in which they can demonstrate their understanding of the content. Create a sample assessment, then model it for a colleague.

3. **Graphic organizers:** There are several graphic organizer websites that offer a significant number of free templates that can be used with newcomers. Explore several sites with free templates and choose a few to use with your students. Create a completed graphic organizer for a topic you currently teach or will teach in the future. Include a word bank of key terms to be "mined" by students to help them complete a blank organizer with a partner or group. Then share your product with colleagues and discuss which works best for different content learning scenarios—literature, mathematics, science, social studies, or even health and/or music lessons. Typical graphic organizers are:

- Frayer model
- Flow chart
- KWL
- T-chart
- Venn diagram
- Concept map

CHAPTER FOUR

Physical, Social, Emotional, and Educational Supports for Newcomers

Best Practice Number Four: Provide supports that address the physical, social, emotional, and educational challenges of newcomers.

For too many years, schools focused mainly on the academic growth of students, often to the exclusion of the other aspects of the individual. Schools are now realizing that academics is only one component of a well-rounded and healthy individual. Supporting the whole child is a concept that has grown in strength across the country in the last few decades, and nowhere is it more critical than with newcomers.

Simply moving from one location to another and entering a new school can be traumatic for any child, but for students who are now in a new country, often with a new language and culture, it can be overwhelming. Most will be experiencing culture shock and will need time and attention as they move through the typical stages of adjustment: euphoria, distress, adjustment, and acceptance. Each student will go through these stages in different lengths of time and will manifest their emotions in different ways, and some individuals skip some stages. While many students may make the adjustment in a few months with the help of their family, friends, and school staff, a good number of students will need additional time and support.

All too often, these students are simultaneously dealing with additional issues and challenges. They may be physically separated from their family, as is the case of unaccompanied minors, losing even that layer of support. These students, and most refugee students as well, are probably suffering post-traumatic stress due to all the dramatic changes in their young lives. "The journey to the United States for these children is often treacherous and traumatic, wrought with a great deal of danger and violence. Many of these children have had traumatic and often violent experiences making that trip, including physical or sexual abuse, days without food, and other horrendous experiences" (Yzquierdo, 2017, p. 41). For students who have experienced trauma in their earlier lives, school may be the place where they feel the most safe and secure. The routines and physical protection of the school may provide hope for a better future. However, other students may need professional help to overcome their fears and insecurity or to find ways to release frustration and anger without resorting to aggression and violence. Schools need to have a plan in place for how to support students who need extra assistance with overcoming traumatic experiences because the need may manifest itself in an emergency situation without warning.

Other common issues that newcomers may be facing include poor self-esteem, insecurity, and a fear of the future. This can lead some students to become dependent or demanding in a bid for attention. Children, especially adolescents, judge themselves by the impressions of their peers, and peers can often be cruel to anyone who is new or different. For students who already feel out of place and uncomfortable, the critical comments of their peers can add one more layer of fear and frustration. On top of the unkind looks and words, newcomers may also experience bullying and even physical abuse. While schools actively try to prevent this, children find ways to avoid detection. Preparing current students for new arrivals before they come and finding ways to help students make friends and create common ground can help to alleviate some of this, although it may be impossible to totally control.

In our previous book, *Supporting the Journey of English Learners after Trauma* (2021), we offer a plethora of suggestions for strategies and activities that can help students make the transition from trauma to resilience. We discuss the importance of creating a trauma-sensitive classroom and school and provide descriptions of classroom activities, such as morning meetings and the use of migration narratives, to guide students through the stages of cultural adjustment. Lisa Auslander (2019), in her book on programming for newcomers titled *Creating Responsive Classroom Communities,* echoes the need for supportive classrooms for students who have experienced trauma before and after their journey to the United States.

> Educator care and emotional support are especially valuable for SLIFE who have suffered through trauma.

Many SIFE have experienced trauma because of violence in their home countries or during their immigration journeys. In addition, especially since many SIFE are refugees or unaccompanied minors, trauma can occur due to unstable or unsafe home situations…Trauma can be a factor in the adolescent lives of SIFE and newcomer students and one that needs to be addressed with skill and care. (Auslander, 2019, p. 8)

Newcomers Who Are Dually Identified

Identifying newcomers who appear to need special education services is challenging, especially considering the well-documented history of over- and under-representation of multilingual learners in special education services, and it continues to remain a concern for educators (*Newcomer Toolkit*, 2023, p. 61). It is important before referral for special education evaluation that language issues, cultural differences, and the typical stages of the language acquisition process be explored. In addition, if a language disorder or disability is suspected, you may use an early intervention approach, such as response to intervention (RTI) or MTSS, both evidenced-based practices, to evaluate the appropriateness of assignment to special education. "Both RTI and MTSS models aim to ensure that when a referral to special education is made, it is appropriate and is not due to misinterpretation of language acquisition and/or cultural differences as a learning disability" (Newcomer Toolkit, 2023, p. 61).

One of the first things to consider when taking an early intervention approach is to look at where and what you are observing and decide if it is a language "difference" or the possibility of a language "disorder" or "disability." Table 12 can help with that determination.

Utilizing Multi-Tiered Systems of Support (MTSS) for Newcomers

Both RTI and MTSS share some underlying philosophies, but in practice, the two are different. RTI is part of an MTSS framework. MTSS uses the RTI process to determine academic needs, but MTSS goes further by addressing behavioral, social, and emotional concerns.

RTI has three tiers of instructional strategies. In Tier I, mainstream or TESOL educators can use systematic instruction such as SIOP with

Table 12: Language Difference or Language Disorder

Language Difference—Developmental Errors	Language Disorder and/or Disability
Pronounces English words differently than native speakers but in correct phrase and/or sentence usage, with practice.	Has difficulty pronouncing English **and** native language words and phrases, includes grammatical usage errors in **both** languages.
Switches between native language and English when needed to communicate both social and academic concepts—codeswitching and/or using translanguaging strategies.	Has difficulty communicating academic vocabulary and concepts in **both** native language and English.
With assistance, can connect recent learning of new vocabulary, language, and/or academic information in native language.	Does not remember recent learning in English—vocabulary, language, and/or other academic information—even when practiced multiple times.
Remembers and can express recently learned academic concepts in English accurately. As a newcomer may combine words with gestures, TPR, and/or drawing. Can connect to native language vocabulary.	Has memory issues around learning in native language and unable to explain concepts. Significant gaps in expressing understanding of learned academic material.
When taught classroom routines, rules, and behavioral expectations, follows them more of the time. Can remember when prompted and self-correct behavior.	Does not possess the ability to understand and/or follow classroom routines, rules, and behavior expectations. Does not remember when prompted and modeled. Is often unable to self-correct behavior.
Learns to appropriately respond to facial expressions, hand gestures, and proximity differences between native and new culture and uses them appropriately for each situation.	Is unable to understand and respond appropriately to facial expressions, hand gestures, and proximity differences between native and new culture, even after several explanations.
Summary: Issues in second language that do not manifest themselves in first language will improve over time with practice when learning new concepts and vocabulary and with social and academic experiences in the second language.	Summary: Disabilities are not language bound; they appear in all languages and social and academic spoken/written experiences of the newcomer.

carefully designed, research-based lesson planning and assessment strategies to teach newcomers. Language objectives focus on the language of the lesson, both vocabulary and language/sentence structures. Building background and activating prior knowledge are part of each lesson and assist teachers in understanding what needs to be differentiated for newcomers and other learners. Assessments at the Tier 1 level are often focused on assessing English language growth. If there are significant gaps in learning, the newcomer is placed in a Tier 2 small group for focused language and academic learning but still maintains inclusion in the general Tier 1 class.

Tier 2 is added for a smaller group of newcomers who need specifically focused supports and strategies, specialized instructional newcomer materials, and/or a specialized small group social and behavioral learning environment. The group could allow more time on tasks, help break down tasks into mini-lessons, and allow for more small group attention and feedback. Progress is checked on a regularly scheduled basis to ensure that learning is taking place.

When neither Tier 1 nor Tier 2 strategies are helping the newcomer make progress in a timely manner, Tier 3 is implemented with specifically targeted strategies for the distinct learning needs of the individual newcomer. Newcomers continue in the mainstream classes with the Tier 1 age/grade group but are given additional, intense interventions with only a few other newcomers needing focused instruction, including perhaps one-to-one assistance. Progress is checked on a regular basis. At this point in the RTI or MTSS process, the newcomer would be or could be evaluated for having a learning disability, when limited progress in learning and retaining the new learning is noted.

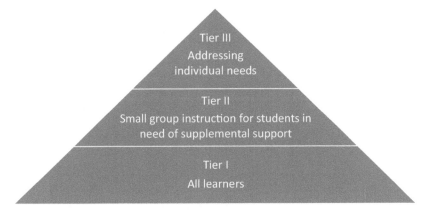

Figure 7: Response to Intervention (RTI) Model

MTSS is a service delivery model that incorporates the three tiers described in RTI, but MTSS may or may not include special education. Along with intensive instructional interventions, MTSS "aims to establish systemwide structures that aid in removing challenges and barriers that may hinder student success" (*Newcomer Toolkit*, 2023, p. 62). These could include professional development for all educators working with newcomers, the involvement of families and family support for newcomers, and community partnerships, such as mental health services, social services, positive behavior intervention and supports, technology tools, and cultural services. With the implementation of RTI and MTSS, teachers could include at Tiers 1 and 2 accommodations in instruction to improve comprehensible input to support student language output. At Tier 3 and beyond, modifications in instructional expectations are used to support student learning. Instruction at Tier 3 can be different from Tiers 1 and 2 by being more frequent and/or being delivered in a different format or learning style, in a smaller group, or even individually.

Components of MTSS

The following core components are key aspects of most MTSS frameworks (based on professional development modules developed by California State University of Los Angeles [2016] and available on their website):

1. **High-quality, differentiated classroom instruction for all students.** This instruction is standards based, differentiated for diverse learners, and carried out by highly qualified teachers who use evidence-based strategies, such as Universal Design for Learning.
2. **Systemic and sustainable change.** This calls for continuous improvement processes at all levels of the system (grade or course level teams, school site teams, district teams).
3. **Integrated data systems.** School and district staff collaborate to create an integrated data collection system that is not limited to state tests but includes universal screenings, diagnoses, progress monitoring data, teacher observations, and parent surveys for continuous systemic improvement.

Dr. Catherine Collier, director of Cross-Cultural Development Education Services and nationally recognized expert on diverse English learners, sees a place for both systems:

Overall, both systems, RTI and MTSS, really encourage interventions that are systematic and research-based (as well as documented) to help students who may need something different than their peers. The data acquired from the processes will help truly identify a student. In the world of our ESL students, this process is crucial to ensure the proper interventions are happening and the language needs are being targeted. This is one step to help with the over-identifying of second language students. I tell my staff to try not to get hung up on acronyms and work to collect a body of evidence that allows for us to the see the whole child, what interventions have occurred and how the student responded to those interventions to help the team move forward with the best approach for the child. (Collier, 2023)

Once a student is identified as needing additional services, what next? As we mentioned earlier, newcomers (and all English learners) must be provided with the opportunity to receive all services for which they qualify. That means that if they are identified as needing special education, and they are still identified as qualifying for English language services as well, that they must be provided *both* services. It is not an either/or situation. The school district must find a way for the student to have support for both their language needs and their learning differences. This

Table 13: Accommodations and Modifications for English Learners with Special Needs

Accommodations	Modifications
Do not fundamentally alter or lower expectations or standards in instructional level, content, or performance criteria	***Do*** fundamentally alter or lower expectations or standards in instructional level, content, or performance criteria.
Changes are made to provide equal access to learning and equal opportunity to demonstrate what is known or understood.	Changes are made to provide student meaningful and productive learning experiences based on independent needs and abilities.
Accommodations in instruction are more qualitative than quantitative	Modifications in instruction are both qualitative and quantitative.
Small group and individual student centered	Individual student centered
Grading is the same for all learners	Grading is different for newcomers while using modifications

could be through a teacher who is dual-certified, but that is extremely rare. Most districts will offer the student support through both special education and ESL/TESOL departments. Ideally, both teachers will have some training in working with dually-identified students. The chart above can offer some suggestions on how to provide accommodations and/or modifications in lessons and lesson delivery. Both teachers must follow the legal requirements as listed in the individual education plan (IEP) for the student.

Addressing Student Physical, Social, and Emotional Needs

One of the best ways to support newcomers with various non-academic needs is to offer services within the school. This type of programming is sometimes referred to as offering "wrap-around services" or creating a "community school." Both terms describe a school that goes beyond the typical academic and extracurricular activities offered by most schools. The idea of establishing a school where families can also receive services such as food, clothing, medical help, and mental health support is a growing phenomenon across the country. A national organization for community schools called the Coalition for Community Schools has this mission on their website (communityschools.org): "The community schools strategy transforms a school into a place where educators, local community members, families, and students work together to strengthen conditions for student learning and healthy development. As partners, they organize in- and out-of-school resources, supports, and opportunities so that young people thrive." According to their website, they already serve about 5,000 schools and are actively recruiting additional partners, both schools and community organizations.

The idea behind these community schools is that the school building should be seen as a community center and a community asset. During and after regular school hours, the location should be able to provide services, such as mental health counseling, a food pantry and clothes closet, a meeting site for families and students, a safe space for after school activities, a place with internet for connectivity, and even medical, dental, and vision services if possible. Families are often more willing to access services that they see as connected to the school (especially mental health services), services they may shy away from in more distant and unfamiliar settings. Utilizing the school as a true public building also makes economic sense and can provide services at a free or reduced cost to families in need.

> It is critical that when you are working with students who are dealing with the aftermath of trauma that you intentionally focus on care for yourself as well. Supporting individuals who have experienced trauma can be emotionally and physically draining, and you cannot help others unless you are taking care of yourself as well.

Many ESL teachers are the main people students turn to for help, not only for academic questions but also for social/emotional fears, worries, and anxieties. It is important that multilingual educators work with others in their buildings to form teams (grade level or content area) to be available to students for their non-academic concerns. Students need to know there is a team there to listen and support the multilingual learner. Knowledge of the ESL population is important for all the members of the team. The team should work together and share their concerns about any student who is experiencing some social/emotional concerns. The team should meet regularly to discuss all the at-risk students and reach out to the school guidance counselor and/or school social worker as needed.

Staffing a Newcomer Program

The Importance of a Trained Staff

Whether or not your school or school district is able to provide the types of wrap-around services mentioned above, it is still vital that trained and caring professionals are available throughout the school to form a network of supports for your new arrivals. These individuals include, but are not limited to, administrators, office personnel, a school nurse, a school psychologist, counselors, graduation coaches, bus drivers, security personnel, family ambassadors or liaisons, and bilingual paraprofessionals. Each one serves as part of a safety net for these vulnerable youth.

> **Caring and trained teachers**—If the newcomer program is composed of one or two teachers as part of a larger school language program, then the focus may be on bilingual or ESL teachers with knowledge and experience working with beginning level students. However, if a separate site or a large, multi-year site is being planned, then staff may need to have certification in specific content areas as well as knowledge of second language learners and learning. Each state has different requirements for working with

ELs. Most require some type of license or certificate when working with language learners, and some, like California and Florida, have requirements that all teachers have training in this area. In California the requirement is called Specially Designed Academic Instruction in English (SDAIE) and is part of the prerequisite for credentialing. Since these requirements change often, it is necessary to check with the state board of education when hiring for a new program.

Administrators—Next to the teachers, probably the most important position in a newcomer program is the administrator. This person will be making the day-to-day decisions that keeps the program running, from selecting staff to creating the master schedule. Without leaders who understand the issues (both academic and non-academic) that newcomers face, the struggle to provide the appropriate services will be much more difficult. Creating a welcoming atmosphere, finding and training the best staff available, creating a schedule that works for the students, and fighting for adequate funding requires administrators who understand the unique needs of newcomers and who care enough to make sure those needs are met. In addition, finding an administrator with experience working with culturally and linguistically diverse students and their families is critical. Ideally, this person will have knowledge of second language acquisition methodology and have connections with the ethnic communities in the area. A positive working relationship with the rest of the school district is also very important, since the newcomers may be coming from multiple buildings and communication will be vital (see Table 14).

Office staff—Often the first faces that newcomers and their families see as they enter a school building are of the office staff. Individuals who are familiar with and comfortable with cross-cultural interactions can make a strong and positive first impression. It is even better when there are individuals who either speak the home language of the new arrivals or who have easy access to someone who does.

Security/campus police—These employees also may interact with families and students when they first enter a new building. While security guards are obviously in place for the protection of the students and staff, it is important for the school to make every effort to put the family and students at ease. Many newcomers

Table 14: Administrator Classroom Observation Checklist

Administrator Classroom Observation Checklist Criteria	Not Observed	Rarely	Sometimes	Often	Always Present
Standards and lesson objectives in easy-to-read language					
Simple, quick assessment of prior knowledge at beginning of lesson					
Lesson begins with building background knowledge and tapping into students' own funds of knowledge					
Introduction of key vocabulary					
Strategic use of first language, whenever possible					
Teacher uses short sentences and repetition					
Strong use of visuals, gestures, and modeling throughout the lesson					
Creative use of supplementary material to scaffold learning					
Assessment that matches the linguistic level of the student					

come from countries where they had good reason to fear or distrust anyone in a uniform, so training security to expect this type of reaction may help prevent problems.

School nurse—This is also someone who may need special training in working with newcomers from various cultures. Many newcomers come from areas of the world where rare diseases may have been prevalent. The students may have been exposed to tuberculosis or have been vaccinated with the BGC tuberculosis vaccine, which often causes a positive skin test, resulting in a chest x-ray being required. Others may be on long-term medication to combat an earlier exposure to tuberculosis. Students arriving with vision, hearing, and dental issues are common. Nurses also need to be aware of the implications of a student's immigration status. Refugees qualify for medical assistance, parolees may or may not depending on status, and undocumented children usually do not have access to medical insurance. However, they do have access to community health clinics where immigration status is not relevant. At times, one child will have a different status than a sibling. Of course, schools are not always aware of a child's immigration status because they are not permitted to ask! Discovering who needs help and what kind they qualify to receive can require a lot of detective work on the part of the school nurse.

School psychologists—These community members can be extremely helpful for students who exhibit evidence of cognitive delay, gifted abilities, or learning disabilities in reading, math, or writing. There are several assessments that can be used with newcomers that are either available in some languages (especially Spanish) or are less language heavy, as well as an array of nonverbal tests usable at every grade level. School psychologists who work with English learners, and especially with newcomers, need to be aware of various methods for identifying learning issues other than the traditional assessments that are used with native English speakers. ELs may have difficulty not only with the vocabulary of the assessments but also with the potential cultural bias of the tests.

Counselors—Counselors wear many hats and can be critical to the support of newcomers. A school counselor can often be the most important non-teaching staff person in the building for many newcomers. They are called the "first responders" for these learners, helping with the lowest two tiers of Maslow's hierarchy: physiological needs, such as food and shelter, and also health and safety needs (Auslander, 2019, p. 33). When trained to work in cross-cultural situations, they can be a vital part of the safety network for newcomers. They fill many roles and can serve as a bridge between the stress of school and the challenges that the student may be facing on a personal level. Below is a non-exhaustive list of ways that counselors can support newcomers. Many items on this list come from a document developed by the Minnesota Department of Education (2010) titled *Working with Refugee Students in Secondary Schools: A Counselor's Companion*. While a small portion of the document is dated and it has a focus on refugee children, the majority remains an excellent guide for a school counselor in supporting English learners. Counselors can and do:

- Serve as caring adult role models and active listeners to the newcomer.

- Aid the student in negotiating the process of acculturation.

- Evaluate school documents, including transcripts, to help the student select the courses needed to work toward graduation.

- Actively review the child's academic success and educational process, encouraging them to stay in school and complete their secondary schooling.

- Help to create an organizational and staff culture that embraces and values diversity and different cultural norms.

- Recognize and respond when students exhibit behaviors of concern that might be indicative of depression, drug use, an inability to manage anger and aggression, and involvement with anti-social groups, such as gangs, or in breaking the law.

- Become knowledgeable about and create linkages with cultural intermediaries and organizations that serve refugee and immigrant families. They can identify therapists in the community who are experienced working with immigrant children and are well-versed in trauma treatment, referring students and families, when necessary.

- Are flexible and creative in meeting the child's and family's needs.

- Involve and support the child's family or caretaker, drawing on them as resources to facilitate the child 's positive development and providing them with support and referrals to services that help them successfully adapt to the United States.

- Engage refugee and immigrant youth, family, and community leaders in designing, running, and/or guiding supplemental programs.

- Assist students and their families when considering post-secondary options and guide the navigation of the complex college admission process, including completing and submitting the free application for federal student aid (FAFSA) form.
- Explore the existence of documents that show the curriculum of the child's home country.

TESOL International acknowledged the vital role of school counselors by publishing the book *Preparing School Counselors for English Language Learners* (Oliveira and Morris, 2015), in which the authors list suggestions for better preparing counselors to work with multilingual learners. They specifically suggest providing counselors with a greater knowledge base of second language development and cultural diversity during their pre-service training. The authors believe that the more the counselors understand their students, the better they will be able to provide proper academic and social-emotional support.

A **graduation coach** is a relatively new role in many schools and school districts. This person often works in conjunction with the high school guidance counselor to assist students to understand the graduation process, which varies from state to state and sometimes from district to district. While the state sets the guidelines for graduation (number of credits or hours, internships required, state assessment requirements, age limits, etc.), it is up to the school to work with students to help them complete their individual graduation plan. A coach helps students understand how credits and GPAs (grade point averages) work, explains options for retaking courses the student may have failed, helps them find tutoring if needed, helps them think about college and career options (including whether vocational courses during high school may be of interest), and explains the role of extracurricular activities and how they can impact grant and scholarship opportunities. And finally, in areas where service-learning hours are required for graduation, coaches can help locate situations where the newcomers can begin to earn hours and can show newcomers how to track this time.

The importance of having **bilingual personnel** throughout the building cannot be overemphasized. When possible, the ideal would be to have employees who fill a typical school role (office staff, teacher, nurse, guidance counselor, etc.) who also speak the language of at least some of the students. However, this is obviously often not possible, especially in a school with multiple language and cultural groups. One alternative is to have individuals on staff, or on call, who can serve as translators or interpreters as needed. This may mean that they work at the district level and visit each school in turn, or it may require hiring a translation/interpretation service that the district pays for on an hourly basis. Many of these district employees are often paraprofessionals who may serve multiple roles for the district. They may work in the enrollment center part of the time, may be available for parent meetings on academic or behavioral conferences, and may also help with after school parent activities. When these individuals serve as interpreters for meetings where legal issues such as disciplinary action or potential placement in special education are being discussed, the interpreter should be trained to just translate and **not** give opinions. The interpreters also need to understand the ramifications of the meetings so that they can give parents information on their rights and responsibilities. And finally, they need to stay neutral in these sometimes very emotional situations and be reminded that what is said in these meetings is private and should not be shared with anyone else, in the building or in the community. The role of the bilingual interpreter/translator is very important and should be treated with respect by the staff and the community.

Another valuable role that is played by paraprofessionals is that of cultural informant. While this may sound like a person who is secretly helping the FBI, it is a term that comes from cultural anthropology. A cultural informant is someone who works with a researcher to explain why people in the culture being studied do what they do. For example, a cultural informant for a student newly arrived from a refugee camp may explain that children run to the cafeteria and push to get to the front of the line because this was a survival technique in the camp.

Having people from the cultures of the students serves many purposes. They are role models for students who often see few people from their background in roles of authority. Often the paraprofessional has strong ties to the immigrant community and knows the families of the students. They can serve as a bridge between the school and the family as well as the ethnic community as a whole. And finally, they serve as cultural informants to the family and community as they work to explain how the school system operates and the expected role of the parent in that system.

Finding qualified paraprofessionals is not an easy task. Many new culture groups, especially those coming from refugee camps or other war-torn areas, may not have the documents to prove educational background. And the few who have the documents are in high demand by many competing organizations. School systems often cannot provide competitive salaries to these groups. Paraprofessionals in school settings are often required to have specialized knowledge of the vocabulary used in situations such as IEP meetings, discipline hearings, physical and mental health issues, etc. And finally, a paraprofessional must have a desire and an aptitude to work with children, probably the most important criteria of all.

Non-certificated personnel who are trained and sensitive to the needs of newcomers, such as cafeteria workers, custodians, and bus drivers

While often overlooked, cultural training for all personnel associated with newcomers is invaluable. These individuals encounter the students daily and can help make English learners' transition to the new school easier or much more difficult. Letting these school employees know about the religious and cultural backgrounds of new arrivals can give them information about food choices, cultural mores, and norms. For example, school cafeterias need to know about the food restrictions of Muslims and Hindus, bus drivers are impacted by which cultures try to separate boys and girls, and playground aides need to know how culture may impact how children socialize on the playground (proximity, holding hands, etc.) and resolve conflict. Custodians are often faced with unhealthy bathroom situations due to the habits of children from areas with poor plumbing who are taught not to place tissue in the toilet. When faced with a stall with no trash can, students may put the paper on the floor. Other students come from areas with sinks designed for washing feet before prayer; when these are not available, they may use the hand sink with disastrous results. A heads up to the custodian and a short discussion with the students can prevent these types of problems.

In Chapter Five, we will cover how best to involve the family and community in the education of newcomers.

Self-Study or Group Study Activities

1. Review the Administrator Classroom Observation Checklist. Are there any additional items you would include in the checklist? Create an additional list of items and describe why these should be included for your administrator to note the quality of instruction for the newcomers in your school. Discuss these with colleagues and revise the list.
2. Professional development usually focuses on the teachers who will be working with the newcomers in their classrooms. However, professional development for the school nurse, custodians, cafeteria workers, bus drivers, and security personnel is often overlooked. Design a series of topics to be covered in a PD session for these essential school personnel who often interact with EL newcomers but know little about their culture and their

limited English language ability. What do each of these school personnel need to know about this new population so that misunderstandings can be avoided?

3. A recent newcomer in your school is from South America. He has made the harrowing journey across the Darién Gap in Panama and witnessed a lady lose her baby as she crossed a swollen river. The middle school child still has nightmares about this event and has trouble sleeping. His mother has asked for help, because the family does not have medical insurance and is having difficulty finding free counseling. Which individuals in your school would be able to aid and support this family? Discuss with colleagues the plan you and other school personnel would devise to provide assistance.

CHAPTER FIVE

Family and Community Supports

Best Practice Number Five: Work with families and communities to support students outside of the school environment.

> Immigrant and refugee families in the United States might not know enough about the US education system and its norms to support their children in US schools, and they might not know what expectations the US school system has for how parents engage with their child's learning. (*Newcomer Toolkit*, 2023, p. 6)

Building partnerships among the child, the school, and the world beyond is important for all students, but for newcomers it can be even more critical. Often, the network of supports that surrounds a child is a combination of family, immediate community including neighborhood friends, their faith community, and cultural ties. For so many newcomers, this safety net has been seriously depleted and needs to be rebuilt. This can also be the case for the adults in the family, who are facing the same culture shock and disorientation that is disturbing the child. Until the adults can find their new equilibrium, they may be less able to offer help to their children. They may be struggling to meet the basic needs of their immediate family and may not have the emotional, financial, or time resources to focus on the myriad needs of their children.

The school can be a lifeline to both the children and the family during this transition, offering information and connections to social services as well as serving as a bridge to the supports available in the community.

Developing and Sustaining Family Partnerships

> Establishing district or school policies and practices that are asset-based and offer a warm and affirming welcome to newcomer students and their families has long-term benefits for the students, their families, and the school community. When newcomer families feel welcomed, they are more apt to engage with their children's schools and teachers. Greater family engagement and involvement lead to positive relationships between immigrant families and the school and, ultimately, to better student outcomes. (*Newcomer Toolkit*, 2023, p. 21)

Building the bridge between school and home can be challenging but worthwhile.

Families come with personal and cultural barriers that may need to be navigated.

Listed below are some of the barriers or challenges developed from past experiences and cultural norms that may impede family involvement:

- Fear of government intervention, especially for families with immigration status instability
- Embarrassment at lack of previous education or level of English proficiency
- Transportation issues
- Parent work schedules that penalize absences, hindering their ability to attend school functions
- Communication and school culture gaps, including not knowing which events are the most important and why.

In addition, families may not be sure if they are welcome or how they can help. These are serious concerns that may take time and multiple contacts to overcome. Translated welcome videos with basic school or district information are one way to introduce families to the new school system. Schools can also look for small ways to include the family in school events at first or allow families to share their expertise in multicultural nights as ice breakers before moving to more time-intensive activities. It is important to remember that it is seldom, if ever, a lack of desire that keeps families from being more active in the school life of their children. "Oftentimes a newcomer's parents' lack of involvement at school is misinterpreted as parents not being interested in their child's education. Depending on the country of origin, parents of immigrant students often hold the teacher and the school in such high regard that they will not interfere with either. Parents will keep their distance, deferring entirely to the authority of the school and the teachers" (Yzquierdo, 2017, p. 31).

At times educators use the terms "family involvement" and "family engagement" interchangeably, but in fact there is an important distinction. "An **involved parent** takes part in the activities already determined by the school. An **engaged parent** takes a step further, often becoming part of the school's decision-making process" (The Annie M. Casey Foundation, 2023). The term "family engagement" is the term used in the current reauthorization of the Elementary and Secondary Education Act (ESSA), known as Every Student Succeeds Act. The distinction is critical. Schools are now mandated to work with families to find more and better ways to work together to support children. The challenge becomes how to create avenues and opportunities to find out what families need and how to utilize their strengths and their funds of knowledge. Families know best what their children need to feel welcome and respected and how to meet those needs in a culturally sensitive manner.

Here are a few ways that schools can work with parents to be more engaged and take the initiative to make themselves as welcoming as possible.

- Have "Meet the Teacher" nights based on the languages of the students to ensure interpreters are present. Share information such as services available, value of regular attendance, parental expectations, suggestions for parental support, etc.
- Bring the community into the school with international nights or culture share days. This has the added benefit of allowing families to share their cultural knowledge with the school in an assets-based manner.
- Provide oral invitations for parents who are not literate through phone calls or digital messages such as Talking Points or WhatsApp, or home visits, when feasible.
- Create a family center in the school with comfortable seating where families, including newcomer families, can meet informally. Include books in newcomers' languages that can be loaned to families to encourage early literacy.
- Offer childcare for parent events.

Schools can also offer workshops or videos on relevant topics to build parent and staff capacity in family partnerships. These workshops could include topics like: how to build an effective school-family team, information on school policies in parent-friendly language, educational programs and services available in the school or community, and information on extracurricular activities and sports (what is available, when and where, cost involved, and how to enroll children). Finally, schools can host a discussion about health and safety issues and share how the school is addressing these issues.

It is important to remember that parents have the right to obtain school information in a language that they understand. The US Department of Education and the Office for Civil Rights published a joint document, known as the Dear Colleague Letter, in January 2015 stating that: "Schools must communicate information to limited English proficient parents in a language they can understand about any program, service, or activity that is called to the attention of parents who are proficient in English" (Dear Colleague Letter, 2015, p. 37). This communication may take the form of translated documents or providing a free interpretation service for phone calls, meetings, or parent conferences. This document includes the following non-exhaustive list of possible areas where translators/interpreters might be needed (p. 38):

- registration and enrollment into school and school programs
- report cards
- student discipline policies and procedures
- special education services, including meetings to discuss potential placement
- parent-teacher conferences
- grievance or discipline procedures
- parent handbooks
- gifted and talented programs
- magnet and charter schools options
- requests for parent permission for student participation in school activities

When considering how best to engage and support newcomer families, it is necessary to keep in mind that not all newcomers arrive with or are living with a nuclear family. Some came to the United States without adult supervision, some are living with extended family or friends, and some may be placed with a sponsor or in a group home. Sensitivity to the home life of the newcomer can help to ease the transition to their new living situation.

Collaborating with Community Organizations

Another invaluable source of support for all students is the plethora of community organizations that are willing and able to offer services to assist children and families in both academic and non-academic areas. Many of these organizations can come into the school, both during and outside of regular school hours. Some provide individual and small group tutoring, English classes, homework help, and mentoring. Others provide what is commonly referred to as "wrap-around" services, such as food and clothing assistance, health care, counseling, and even legal aid.

> There is a range of community organizations schools may partner with, such as arts or cultural organizations, mental health centers, religious organizations, refugee resettlement agencies, and post-secondary education institutions (e.g., community colleges, career and technical programs, and universities). Many school-community partnerships center around health, mental health, and social services (e.g., housing assistance, food banks, job centers). When choosing which organizations to partner with, schools should consider the needs of the newcomer families, as well as the availability, mission, ability, and interest of the organizations. (*Newcomer Toolkit*, 2023, p. 31)

How Community Organizations Can Support Newcomers

> Mentoring: many groups offer individual tutoring and mentoring for school age students, including service organizations, faith-based organizations, colleges/universities, and Big Brothers, Big Sisters. The obvious benefit of mentoring is that the mentor develops a relationship with the mentee; they can provide the student with not just academic assistance but also cultural adjustment and emotional support. For newcomers, it is especially helpful if the mentoring can occur at the school or else close to where the student lives, since they are still learning to navigate their new environment.
>
> Homework help: Many organizations also offer homework help, either at the school or at a separate location. Public libraries in many cities now offer homework help provided by either volunteers or paid library staff. Many libraries also offer free literacy and/or ESL classes for adults, preparing them for the national citizenship test or for the GED test. The library is a

central location that appeals to many families because it is safe, free, religiously neutral, and encourages reading and computer access for the whole family.

Expanded Learning Opportunities: Many schools provide students the chance to stay after school or come on weekends for school-sponsored activities, which may focus on academic assistance or just fun programming. These often go by the acronym ELO, which stands for "expanded learning opportunities." School staff or school facilities also provide a safe, familiar environment for newcomers.

Other organizations offer students the opportunity to participate in after school **sports**, **crafts**, and **cultural activities**. Local sports teams may sponsor camps or even tryouts for youth teams, the parks and recreation department frequently provides art-related events for all ages, and music and drama organizations often visit schools to introduce students to various cultural activities.

Most ethnic groups create local organizations to promote ethnic pride and share **cultural events** such as dances, food, art, and heritage language classes. Some newcomer families may not yet be aware of these groups in their own community and the many services and benefits they offer, so connecting new arrivals with these groups is one action that bilingual or ESL personnel can provide.

Other area organizations that may visit the school or be a perfect location for a field trip are **science museums, zoos, municipal or state parks, history centers**, etc. Most of these entities have an educational component and some even have traveling exhibits or mobile vans. When arranging for newcomers to participate, it is a good idea to prepare the docents or presenters with a few tips in advance, such as using lots of visuals, speaking slowly, and perhaps even offering translators.

Summer is the perfect time to provide extra services to newcomers. English classes or summer school would be especially beneficial, but also **summer camps** of any type will give new arrivals the opportunity to build friendships, familiarize themselves with their new community, learn new skills or hone previous ones, and destress before a new academic year. "Camp" does not necessary mean going away from home; it can be a few hours in the school, a park, or a recreation center.

One final excellent use of outside organizations is as a placement location for students to earn **service-learning hours** or even participate in an internship. Some schools and some states require a certain number of hours for graduation, and for students to be able to begin logging these hours in a location in which a higher level of English proficiency is not expected can be invaluable. Some schools find opportunities for students to become familiar with this expectation and to begin banking hours within the school, doing such work as serving as a "buddy" for newer arrivals, acting as a student helper in the classroom, cleaning the lunchroom, making photocopies, decorating bulletin boards, or tutoring younger students, etc.

How to Get Connected to Community Organizations

If you have students who come to your community as refugees, the local refugee resettlement organization is required to connect with the school through quarterly community meetings. Any entity that is impacted by refugees is invited to these consultations: health care providers, landlords, municipal leaders, food banks, job and family services, and schools. If your school district has not been invited, contact the refugee organization directly or go through the state coordinator for information on these meetings.

Most local cultural centers and civic organizations are very interested in collaborating with schools and will welcome opportunities to share their passion with students. The same is true for public libraries. Introducing students and their families to this invaluable resource can be one of the most important connections to be made. And finally, many faith-based organizations are looking for ways to serve their communities and are eager to support their local schools.

Self-Study or Group Study Activities

1. The school district of Palm Beach County in Florida created a brochure, available in multiple languages, about the health and social services available in their county as well as those available in their enrollment Welcome Center: school registration, school placement, meal applications, vaccinations, transcript evaluation, as well as counseling and social service referrals if needed. They also connected with the local Mayan association for specialized supports for their families who spoke a dialect of the Mayan language.

   Think about ways in which your own school district and local elementary, middle, and high schools could replicate what Palm Beach County has done. Work with others in your school, including administration, and the community to find these resources and create your own specific brochure. Outreach beyond teachers could include members of the parent-teacher organization and members of the local board of education (Ortolazo, 2023).

2. Connecticut has two organizations that provide resettlement help for refugees: the Connecticut Institute for Refugees and Immigrants (https://cirict.org), which provides legal, economic, linguistic, and social services to immigrants, refugees, and unaccompanied minors, and Integrated Refugee & Immigrant Services (https://irisct.org), which provides services to and for undocumented immigrants and cultural groups such as Cubans, Haitians, and Ukrainians. They work to help new immigrants find housing, furniture, goods, and toiletries and have a pantry to help prevent food insecurity for all clients they serve. They also have a marketplace, which helps to provide household items, kitchen supplies, toys, and books for children.

   Think about ways in which your own school district and local elementary, middle, and high schools could replicate what Connecticut has done. Work with others in your school and community to find organizations that would be willing to partner with you and create your own specific brochure of resources. Who could best work on this research and create a brochure? Reach out to others in your local education agency (LEA), including administrators, guidance counselors, the parent-teacher organization, and the local board of education to assist with this.

3. A local woman's group in Northern California decided to create a student store for elementary children, grades 1 to 3, in their local school district. They reached out to several local big box stores for donations of multiple sizes of clothing, coats, and backpacks filled with starter school supplies. At the beginning of each school year, classes of children came to the store, managed by the woman's group, who then helped the children choose a set of clothing (shirt, pants, underwear, and socks), a coat, and a backpack filled with supplies. Think of ways that your own school district could do outreach in your community to set up a similar "student store." Who could your team approach? Create a plan with colleagues in your school district.

References and Resources

Introduction

Plyler v. Doe, 457 U.S. 202 (1982). https://supreme.justia.com/cases/federal/us/457/202/

Short, D. and Boyson, B. (2012). *Helping newcomer students succeed in secondary schools and beyond.* Center for Applied Linguistics. https://www.cal.org/wp-content/uploads/2022/06/Helping-Newcomer-Students-Report.pdf

Sugarman, J. (2023). *Recent immigrant children: A profile of new arrivals to U.S. schools.* Migration Policy Institute.

Ventura, J. "America struggles with protecting unaccompanied minors at the border." (2023, July 19, 2023). News Nation Now. https://www.newsnationnow.com/us-news/immigration/border-coverage/unaccompanied-migrant-children-labor-trafficking/#:~:text=In%20the%202023%20fiscal%20year,were%20encountered%20at%20the%20border.

Ward, N. and Batalova, J. (2023, March 14). *Frequently requested statistics concerning immigration in the United States.* Migration Policy Institute. https://www.migrationpolicy.org/article/frequently-requested-statistics-immigrants-and-immigration-united-states

UNHCR. (2022). *UNHCR Refugee Education Report.* https://www.unhcr.org/631ef5a84/unhcr-education-report-2022-inclusive-campaign-refugee-education

Chapter One

Auslander, L. (2019). *Creating responsive classroom communities: A cross-case study of schools serving students with interrupted schooling.* Lexington Books.

Castañeda v. Pickard. 648 F. 2d 989 (1981). https://www.casemine.com/judgement/us/5914c45badd7b049347cd023

Chang, H. (1990). *Newcomer programs: Innovative efforts to meet the educational challenges of immigrant students.* California Tomorrow.

Dear Colleague Letter. (2015, January 7). Washington, DC: United States Department of Education and United States Department of Justice.

DeCapua, A., Smathers, W., and Tang, L. F. (2009). *Meeting the needs of students with limited or interrupted education.* University of Michigan Press.

Friedlander, M. (1991, fall). *The newcomer program: Helping immigrant students succeed in U.S. schools.* Program Information Series Guide, No. 8. National Clearinghouse for Bilingual Education.

Hofstetter, J. & Cherewka, A. (2022, February). *The integrated English literacy and civics education (IELCE) program: Understanding Its design and challenges in meeting immigrant learners' needs.* Migration Policy Institute. https://www.migrationpolicy.org/research/ielce-design-immigrant-learners

Jury, J. (2023, January 30). Personal communication.

Klein, E. C. & Martohardjono, G. (2010). *Students with interrupted formal education: A challenge for the New York City public schools.* Advocates for Children of New York. https://www.advocatesforchildren.org/SIFE%20Paper%20final.pdf?pt=1

McKinney-Vento Homeless Assistance Act. (2015). Title 42, Education of Homeless Children and Youths. https://nche.ed.gov/legislation/mckinney-vento/

Napolitano, J. (2021). *The school I deserve.* Beacon Press.

National Association for Gifted Children. (2019, July 11). "Identifying and serving culturally and linguistically diverse gifted learners." https://cdn.ymaws.com/nagc.org/resource/resmgr/knowledge-center/position-statements/a_definition_of_giftedness_t.pdf

Newcomer Toolkit. (2023, June). United States Department of Education. https://ncela.ed.gov/sites/default/files/2023-09/NewcomerToolkit-09152023-508.pdf

Plyler v. Doe, 457 U.S. 202 (1982). https://supreme.justia.com/cases/federal/us/457/202/

Short. D. and Boyson, B. (2006). *Creating access: Language and academic programs for secondary school newcomers.* Center for Applied Linguistics.

Short, D. and Boyson, B. (2012). *Helping newcomer students succeed in secondary schools and beyond.* Center for Applied Linguistics. https://www.cal.org/wp-content/uploads/2022/06/Helping-Newcomer-Students-Report.pdf

United Stated Department of Education, Office of Career, Technical and Adult Education. https://lincs.ed.gov

Workforce Innovation and Opportunity Act. (2014, July 22). https://www.dol.gov/agencies/eta/wioa

Yzquierdo, M. (2017). *Pathways to greatness for ELL newcomers: A comprehensive guide for schools and teachers.* Seidlitz Education.

Educator Resources

Motamedi, J. Porter, L. Taylor, S, Leong, M. Martinez-Wenzl, M. & Serrano, D. (2021, February). *Welcoming, registering, and supporting newcomer students: A toolkit for educators of immigrant and refugee students in secondary schools.* United States Department of Education. https://files.eric.ed.gov/fulltext/ED610689.pdf

Information on the Internationals Network. https://www.internationalsnetwork.org

Information on the CUNY Bridges to Academic Success project: website bridges-sife.project.com or email info@bridges-sifeproject.com

Information on bullying prevention: https://www.stopbullying.gov

Information on supporting homeless children based on the McKenney-Vento Act. https://nche.ed.gov/legislation/mckinney-vento/

Chapter Two

August, D. & Hakuta, K. (Eds.). (1997). *Improving schooling for language-minority students: A research agenda*. National Academy Press.

August, D. & Shanahan, T. (Eds). (2006). *Developing literacy in second-language learners: Report of the National Literacy Panel on Language-Minority Children and Youth*. Lawrence Erlbaum Associates.

Bialystok, E. (2002). *Acquisition of literacy in bilingual children: A framework for research. Language Learning.* 52 (1), 159–199.

Cárdenas-Hagan, E. (2020). *Literacy foundations for English learners: A comprehensive guide to evidence-based instruction*. Brookes Publishing Company.

Cummins, J., et al. (2006, January). *ELL students speak for themselves: Identity texts and literacy engagement in multilingual classrooms.* University of Toronto Press.

Escamilla, K., Olsen, L. & Slavick, J. (2022). *Toward comprehensive effective literacy policy and instruction for English learner/emergent bilingual students*. National Committee on Effective Literacy. Multilingualliteracy.org. https://multilingualliteracy.org/wp-content/uploads/2022/04/21018-NCEL-Effective-Literacy-White-Paper-FINAL_v2.0.pdf

Krashen, S. (1982). *Principles and practice in second language acquisition.* Prentice-Hall.

National Institute of Child Health and Human Development. (2000). *Report of the National Reading Panel: Teaching children to read.* Washington DC: U.S. Government Printing Office.

Scarborough, H. S. (2001). Connecting early language and literacy to later reading (dis)abilities: Evidence, theory, and practice. In S. Neuman & D. Dickinson (Eds.). *Handbook for research in early literacy* (pp. 97–110). Guilford Press.

Educator Resources

A framework for foundational literacy skills instruction for English learners. (2023). Council of the Great City Schools. https://www.cgcs.org/cms/lib/DC00001581/Centricity/domain/35/publication%20docs/CGCS_Foundational%20Literacy%20Skills_Pub_v11.pdf

Olsen, L. (2022, September). *Comprehensive literacy instruction for English language learners*. National Committee on Effective Literacy. https://multilingualliteracy.org/wp-content/uploads/2022/09/21025-NCEL-Literacy-Model-FINAL.pdf

Park, J. B., Escamilla, K., & Olsen. L. (2022, September 21). *Effective literacy instruction for multilingual learners: What it is and what it looks like.* Webinar. NCELA. https://ncela.ed.gov/events/2022-09-21-webinar-effective-literacy-instruction-for-multilingual-learners-what-it-is-and

Spanish-English Cognate list. ColorinColorado. https://www.colorincolorado.org/sites/default/files/Cognate-List.pdf

Chapter Three

ColorinColorado. (2012, December 13). *Tips for welcoming newcomers.* [Video]. YouTube. https://www.youtube.com/watch?v=uh19gewSNFg&list=PLoU659hwTdDanhjbsztAkszwA_VgKeDey&t=10s.

Freeman Y., Freeman D., Soto M., and Ebe A. (2016). *ESL teaching: Principles for success.* Heinemann.

Garcia, O., Ibarra Johnson, S. & Seltzer, K. (2016). *The translanguaging classroom: Leveraging student bilingualism for learning.* Brookes Publishing.

Gross, H. (2022, November 29). *Five Tips for Co-Teaching.* National Education Association. https://www.nea.org/professional-excellence/student-engagement/tools-tips/5-tips-co-teaching

Hammond, Z. (2014). *Culturally responsive teaching and the brain.* Corwin Press.

Honigsfeld, A. and Dove, M. (2017). *Co-teaching for English learners.* Corwin Press.

Jackson, P. W. (1968). *Life in classrooms.* Holt, Rinehart, Winston.

Jiménez, F. (1997). *The circuit: From the life of a migrant child.* Houghton Mifflin.

Najarro, I. (2023, July 13). What is translanguaging and how is it used in the classroom? *Education Week.* https://www.edweek.org/teaching-learning/what-is-translanguaging-and-how-is-it-used-in-the-classroom/2023/07

Pearson, P. D., & Gallagher, M. C. (1983). The instruction of reading comprehension. *Contemporary Educational Psychology, 8*(3), 317–344. https://doi.org/10.1016/0361-476X(83)90019-X

Yzquierdo, M. (2017). *Pathways to greatness for ELL newcomers: A comprehensive guide for schools and teachers.* Seidlitz Education.

Educator Resources

Co-Teaching Resources

California State University at Chico. (2015, August 9). *Six co-teaching strategies* [Video]. YouTube. https://www.youtube.com/playlist?list=PLCDsTyftAA2D_buI_Rti5phLZ1DdFsAMc

Chapman, C. & Hyatt, C. H. (2011). *Critical conversations in co-teaching: A problem-solving approach.* Solution Tree.

Corwin. (2017, October 25). *Maria Dove & Andrea Honigsfeld: Co-Teaching for English Learners Webinar* [Video].YouTube. https://www.youtube.com/watch?v=zAooVs4U2zA

Council of the Great City Schools. (2013, July 25). *Co-teaching for English Language Learners in NYC* [Video]. YouTube. https://www.youtube.com/watch?v=D7IfQ8oYPBA

Honigsfeld, A. and Dove, M. (2022, February 24) NYSED Topic Brief 4. *Seven Models of Co-Teaching.*

Chapter Four

Auslander, L. (2019). *Creating responsive classroom communities: A cross-case study of schools serving students with interrupted schooling.* Lexington Books.

California State University of Los Angeles. (2016) Professional Development program on MTSS. https://ceedar.education.ufl.edu/mtss-udl-di-dev/MTSSchapterStart.html

Coalition for Community Schools at the Institute for Educational Leadership. (2023, August 2). https://www.communityschools.org

Collier, C. (2023, November 7). Personal communication.

De Oliveira, L. C. and Morris, C. W. (2015). *Preparing school counselors for English language learners.* TESOL International Association.

Minnesota Department of Education. *Working with refugee students in secondary schools: A counselor's companion.* (2010).

Newcomer Toolkit. (2023, June). United States Department of Education. https://ncela.ed.gov/sites/default/files/2023-09/NewcomerToolkit-09152023-508.pdf

O'Loughlin, J. and Custodio, B. (2021). *Supporting the journey of English learners after trauma.* University of Michigan Press.

Yzquierdo, M. (2017). *Pathways to greatness for ELL newcomers: A comprehensive guide for schools and teachers.* Seidlitz Education.

Educator Resources

School Climate Resource

Free School Climate Survey from the USDE to download and administer: https://safesupportivelearning.ed.gov/edscls

Assessment Resources

Video of Lorraine Valdez Pierce discussing assessment on the ColorinColorado website. https://www.colorincolorado.org/webcast/assessment-english-language-learners

Chapter Five

The Annie M. Casey Foundation (2023, February 1). *Parent Involvement vs. Parent Engagement.* The Annie M. Casey Foundation. https://www.aecf.org/blog/parental-involvement-vs-parental-engagement#:~:text=What%20many%20may%20not%20know,the%20school%27s%20decision%2Dmaking%20process

Dear Colleague Letter. (2015, January 7). Washington, DC: United States Department of Education and United States Department of Justice.

Newcomer Toolkit. (2023, June). United States Department of Education. https://ncela.ed.gov/sites/default/files/2023-09/NewcomerToolkit-09152023-508.pdf

Ortolazo, J. (2023, March 8). Personal communication. Palm Beach County School District, Florida.

Yzquierdo, M. (2017). *Pathways to greatness for ELL newcomers: A comprehensive guide for schools and teachers.* Seidlitz Education.

Educator Resources

Family Engagement Resources

ColorinColorado (www.colorincolorado.org) offers several strategies and supports for families on their website through "Engaging ELL Families Through Community Partnerships." The article includes information for key services, including interpreters, medical care, educational opportunities, and ESL, GED, and citizenship classes.

Strategies for Supporting Newcomer and Immigrant Families Navigating the School System. (2023, July 18). Webinar by Welcoming America. https://welcomingamerica.org/resource/strategies-for-supporting-newcomer-and-immigrant-families-navigating-the-school-system/

National Alliance for Family Engagement. https://famengage.org

National Association for Family, School, and Community Engagement. https://nafsce.org

Resources for Mayan Heritage Families

The Guatemalan-Maya Center. Serving families of Mayan descent in the Palm Beach County, Florida, area. https://www.guatemalanmaya.org

International Mayan League. Resources and programing about Mayan history and culture. Washington, DC. https://www.mayanleague.org

Index

Accommodations 29, 66, 70, 73, 81
Administrator Classroom Observation Checklist 85
Annie M. Casey Foundation 95
Asylees 5
August, Diane 36
Auslander, Lisa 26–27, 76–77, 86

Batalova 6
Bialystok 36
Boyson, Beverly 2, 16

California Tomorrow 12, 16, 84, 100
Cardenas-Hagan, Elsa 41
Castaneda v Pickard 23
Center for Applied Linguistics (CAL) 13
Chang, Hedy 12
Chewerka 30
City University of New York (CUNY) 26–27
Co-teaching 69–71
Cognates 63–65, 72
Collier, Catherine 80–81
Community school 82
Comprehensible input 43, 46, 58, 66
Concepts of print 51
Cultural informant 89
Culturally responsive teaching 26, 58
Cummins, Jim 48
Customs and Border Patrol (CBP) 6

Dear Colleague Letter 22–23, 96
DeCapua, Andrea 26
Decoding 38, 51
Disabilities 9, 27, 78, 86
Dove, Maria 70–71
Dually-identified 77, 82

Elementary and Secondary Education Act 95
Escamilla 36
Expanded learning opportunities (ELO) 14, 98

FAFSA 7, 88
Fluency 41, 51
Frayer vocabulary model 50, 62, 74
Friedlander, Monica 12

Garcia, O. 68
Geneva Convention (1951) 5
Gifted and talented 28–29, 96
GPA (grade point average) 88
Gradual Release of Responsibility 67
Graduate Equivalency Degree or General Education Diploma (GED). 33, 97, 106
Graduation coach 88
Graphic organizers 32, 40, 46, 49, 62, 74

Hakuta, Kenji 36
Hammond, Zaretta 58
Hidden curriculum 55–57, 73
Hofstetter 30
Honinsfeld, Andrea 70–71

Ibarra Johnson 68
Individuals with Disabilities Education Act (IDEA) 27
Integrated English Literacy and Civics Education (IELCE) 30
Internationals Network 16, 26, 102

Jackson 55
Jimenez, Francisco 61
Jury, Jamie 22

Klein 26
Krashen, Stephen 43
KWL Chart 61, 72, 74

Language difference 77–78
Language disorder 77–78
LEAs (Local Education Associations) 100
Looping 21
Low incidence 16, 19–22

Index

Manipulatives 48–51, 65–66
Martohardjono 26
Maslow's Hierarchy of Needs 86
McKinney-Vento Act 19, 103
Mentor 97
Migration Policy Institute (MPI) 2
Minnesota Department of Education 87
Modifications 66, 70, 81
MTSS 27, 77–81

Najarro, Ileana 67
Napolitano, Jo 25
National Association for Gifted Children (NAGC) 28
National Committee on Effective Literacy 36
National Education Association 69
National Literacy Panel on Language-Minority Children and Youth 36
National Reading Panel 36
Native, home, or first language 3, 12, 17, 20, 24, 26–28, 41–42, 49, 56–57, 66–68, 72–74, 78, 85
Newcomer Toolkit 27–29, 31, 77, 80, 93–94, 97
Newcomers' definition 1, 4
Numeracy 4, 7, 9, 14, 17, 26, 32, 35, 46–47, 49, 59–60

Office for Civil Rights 22, 96
Olsen, Laurie 36
Ortolazo, Javier 100

Paraprofessionals 15, 17, 21, 83, 89
Parent involvement/parent engagement 94–95
Phonemic awareness 22, 36–37
Phonics 22, 38–39, 46, 51
Plyler v Doe (1982) 5, 18
Political asylum 5–6
Polysemous words 63
Prentice, Amber 54

Reading Rope 44–46
Realia 22, 49–50, 62, 66
Refugees 5, 29, 77, 86, 99, 100
Rosenthal, Roger xii–xiii, 13
RTI 77–81

Scarborough, Hollis 44–45
Self-contained 11, 21
Seltzer 68
Shanahan, Timothy 36
Sheltered Instruction Observation Protocol (SIOP) 50, 77
Short, Deborah 2, 16
SIFE/SLIFE xiii, 3, 25–26, 77
Slavick 36
Smathers, William 26
Sugarman, Julie 2

Tang, Lixing Frank 26
TESOL 77, 82, 88
The Circuit 61
Tier I-III levels of services 35, 77–80
Tier I-III vocabulary words 37
TPR 48, 64, 78
TPR (Total Physical Response) 48, 64, 78
TPS 5
Translanguaging 67–68, 78

Unaccompanied minors 6, 76–77, 100
UNHCR 5
United States Department of Education xi, 22, 105
United States Department of Justice 22

Venn Diagram 62, 74
Visa (types of visas) 4

Ward 6
Workforce Innovation and Opportunity Act (WIOA) 31
Wrap-around services 82

Yzquierdo, Michelle 22, 27, 72, 76, 95